D0444591

CHOOSING BEAUTY

choosing
beauty

a 30-day
spiritual makeover
for women

GINA LOEHR

SERVANT
BOOKS

PUBLISHED BY ST. ANTHONY MESSENGER PRESS
CINCINNATI, OHIO

Cover and book design by Mark Sullivan
Cover photo © istockphoto.com/C W Lawrence

LIBRARY OF CONGRESS CATALOGING-IN-PUBLICATION DATA
Loehr, Gina.
Choosing beauty : a 30-day spiritual makeover for women / Gina Loehr.
p. cm.
Includes bibliographical references.
ISBN 978-0-86716-921-8 (pbk. : alk. paper) 1. Christian women—Religious life. 2. Beauty, Personal—Religious aspects—Christianity. I. Title.
BV4527.L6334 2009
248.8'43—dc22
2009011626

ISBN 978-0-86716-921-8

Published by Servant Books, an imprint of St. Anthony Messenger Press.
28 W. Liberty St.
Cincinnati, OH 45202
www.ServantBooks.org

Printed in the United States of America.

Printed on acid-free paper.

09 10 11 12 13 5 4 3 2 1

For my cousin Jenny

contents

A woman's beauty gladdens the countenance,
and surpasses every human desire.

—Sirach 36:22

Scripture says that of all the things human beings crave, women's beauty tops the list. And our experience supports the idea. We place a high value on feminine beauty: Men love to behold it, and women long to have it.

Why did God make women especially beautiful? Why did he plant a desire for feminine beauty in the hearts of men and women alike?

I believe he did this as a way to reveal himself to us. In the divine design a woman's beauty—her true, authentic beauty—is a gateway to God. Ultimately the thirst for beauty is a thirst for God himself.

I'm not talking about the one-dimensional beauty of the air-brushed supermodels on the covers of *Glamour* and *Vogue*, mind you. I'm talking about the built-in beauty—both physical and spiritual—of *every* woman, you and me included. We were made in the image of God precisely as women. In its fullness our beauty is a reflection of our Creator, the perfect artist who defines beauty itself. Our true beauty shines most clearly when we live in harmony with him.

Choosing Beauty: A 30-Day Spiritual Makeover for Women is for any woman who wants her built-in beauty to flourish. It is structured in thirty brief sections aimed at helping women wholeheartedly embrace their true beauty by cultivating virtue. As such, the book is ideal for personal use over the course of a month. Alternatively you might read *Choosing Beauty* in a discussion group, reflecting with other women on one section per meeting. If the group prefers a faster pace, each woman can read and reflect on an entire chapter during the week, and the meeting time can be spent discussing significant points.

This book is also well suited for mothers who recognize the value of forming their daughters in virtue. Mother and daughter can read and discuss the text together, or if the daughter is young, Mom can read it by herself and then present the ideas in a suitable format.

Youth ministers as well will find the book helpful for encouraging virtue in the young women with whom they work.

Each chapter includes three readings with related prayers and questions for reflection. At the end of each chapter is a suggested spiritual activity as well as space to record your personal reaction and a resolution for how you intend to put the ideas into practice. At the end of the book are seven "Virtuous Victories" sheets to assist you in your personal plan for developing virtue and growing in the fullness of beauty.

In addition to working through the thirty-day format, you may utilize this text as a reference for information about the cardinal and theological virtues, including relevant quotes from Scripture and the *Catechism of the Catholic Church*. I encourage you to keep a copy of the Bible and the *Catechism* handy as you read.

Religious writers and saints offer us considerable insight on the life of virtue, so I have incorporated occasional quotes from them as well. The "Models" section at the end of each chapter shows how Mary and other holy women lived out the particular virtues. My hope is that *Choosing Beauty* will be a useful resource for examples of holy women, more of which you can find in the companion book to this text, *Real Women, Real Saints: Friends for Your Spiritual Journey* (Servant, 2008).

I encourage you to approach this book in a spirit of prayerful reflection. God designed you to quench the thirst of a world desperately longing to behold the glory of authentic beauty. As you begin your spiritual makeover, bear this noble mission in mind. And remember that whenever you choose virtue, you are also choosing beauty.

chapter one

CHOOSING BEAUTY

Day 1: A Spiritual Makeover

I knew I had a problem when I misplaced my cosmetics bag one Ash Wednesday. It was only an hour before I was supposed to lead a retreat, and I couldn't find my makeup anywhere. I was frantic. How could I stand up in front of all those people without any eyeliner? What would they think of me with my cheeks unblushed? I was afraid to share the gospel because I wasn't wearing my mascara.

At some point in the midst of my panic, I realized how ridiculous this was. I was addicted to makeup. I couldn't function normally without it. Earlier that morning I had asked God to show me what I should give up for Lent. Suddenly I knew that I should accept the challenge of living without makeup for the next forty days.

The sacrifice was almost too much to bear, for the first week anyway. I felt ugly and insecure. I avoided mirrors. I made derogatory comments about my appearance before anyone else had a chance to do so.

But as the days wore on, I began to notice a few surprising facts. People still talked to me. They still smiled at me and engaged in conversation with me. The retreats I led went fine. I didn't become the subject of any public ridicule. It began to matter less and less that I wasn't wearing makeup.

By week three I was glad for the extra time I had each morning. And when Lent finally came to an end, I was liberated from my addiction. Finally I could wear makeup if I *wanted* to, but I no longer felt that I *had* to.

This process led me to reflect on how much more concerned I was about my physical beauty than my spiritual beauty. I didn't get frantic after losing my patience; I got frantic after losing my makeup. My lack of charity didn't bother me nearly as much as my lack of face powder. I knew this was imbalanced. I wanted to begin to focus on becoming beautiful inside *and* out.

The simple fact is that no matter how much a woman paints herself, no matter how stylishly she dresses or how well manicured she keeps her nails, no matter how well she does her hair or how much silicone enhances her figure, she will never reach the fullness of her physical beauty until she reaches the fullness of her spiritual beauty. No eye shadow can match the impact of virtue. No lotion can produce the glow of holiness. The radiance of sanctity can be seen, but it can't be bought.

Holiness embellishes our inborn beauty as nothing else can. And this fullness of beauty is freely accessible to everyone. It's all up to us: We can choose to let this beauty flourish, or we can ignore the primary importance of our spiritual life and settle for mediocre, worldly beauty alone.

Scripture gives us a picture of a woman who is the perfect blend of spiritual and physical beauty. These verses speak in the context of marriage, but the ideals apply to all women:

> Like the sun rising in the heights of the Lord,
>> so is the beauty of a good wife in her well-ordered home.
> Like the shining lamp on the holy lampstand,

so is a beautiful face on a stately figure.

Like pillars of gold on a base of silver,

so are beautiful feet with a steadfast heart. (Sirach 26:16–18)

The beauty of a virtuous woman lights up her home, her community, her workplace, "like the sun." She is inherently attractive. This is exactly what so many women long to be. And this longing to be attractive, beautiful even, is planted in our hearts by God. He made us to be beautiful in the fullest sense, inside and out.

Scripture urges women not to reduce beauty by focusing on externals alone but to cultivate spiritual beauty by focusing on the interior virtues. The First Letter of Saint Peter says our adornment should be "the imperishable jewel of a gentle and quiet spirit, which in God's sight is very precious" (1 Peter 3:4).

Becoming a truly virtuous woman will take time and effort, but if we can spend as much time beautifying our souls as we spend beautifying our bodies, we'll be doing well. Over the course of these thirty days, I encourage you to spend a few minutes every day focusing on spiritual beauty by learning concrete ways to develop virtue. If you truly take these reflections to heart and allow them to affect your life, you will be amazed at how much "brighter" your soul will be one month from now. As a woman of authentic beauty, you will begin to light up everything—and everyone—you encounter.

PRAYER

Lord God, as I begin this month of spiritual growth, I need your help. I want to grow into the fullness of beauty, reflecting your glory to the world. Please help me stay committed to this process. Amen.

REFLECTION QUESTIONS

1. Do you ever feel pressure to dress or do your hair in a certain way? Have you ever felt that your self-confidence depended on makeup, beauty tools or cosmetic supplies? How do feelings like these affect your freedom?

2. If someone said that you were beautiful "on the inside," would you be flattered or insulted? Do you agree that your spiritual beauty affects your physical beauty?

3. What does the word *virtue* mean to you?

4. Why do you think a "gentle and quiet spirit" is precious in the sight of God? What standards would you set for femininity that are based on what's true instead of what's trendy?

5. What are some practical ways you can make the most of this month of spiritual growth?

Day 2: How to Be a Virtuoso

When I was in grade school, my dad taught me to play a few songs on the piano. Although this gave me confidence in my musical skill, the songs in my tiny repertoire made me only *appear* to be a piano player. Later, when I actually took lessons, I realized that more effort and discipline would be necessary if I wanted to play for real.

At first the discipline of repeating mundane drills and scales over and over again felt burdensome. I was annoyed that my teacher made me play such ridiculously simple ditties when I could already play full-fledged songs without a hitch. But after mastering the foundational knowledge and skills of reading music, playing the piano became an even greater joy than it had been before.

Once a musician learns to read music well enough, she has the freedom to sight-read anything she'd like to play. Once she has music theory down, she has the freedom to improvise and even compose her own works. And with real dedication to her instrument, she might become a virtuoso, possessing a skill that others will even pay to hear.

But a musician must work to form the good habits that give her the freedom to play her instrument so beautifully. Developing our inner beauty is similar. By forming good spiritual habits (that is, the virtues), we gain the freedom to be spiritually beautiful. We thus become attractive in the fullest sense of the word, as God intended us to be. Just as a skilled violinist displays her musical genius, we reveal our "feminine genius" through our practice of the virtues.

The *Catechism of the Catholic Church* defines virtue as "an habitual and firm disposition to do the good" (*CCC*, 1803). If you have the virtue of justice, for example, you will consistently and easily do what is just: You act justly as a matter of *habit*. But this consistency doesn't come overnight. We establish the virtues through repeated practice. Repetition enables a virtue to take root and become a habit.

Of course, part of forming good habits is getting rid of bad ones. If a piano player stops and groans in frustration every time she makes a mistake, she will have to break that habit before she will ever make it through a piece. Likewise, to grow in virtue we have to get rid of certain weaknesses and patterns of sin. These weaknesses—the opposites of virtues—we call *vices*. By forming the good habits of virtue, we loosen the hold of vices on our souls. If we struggle with a particular vice, we can practice a corresponding virtue to counteract it.

Seven virtues are especially important. They fall into two categories: cardinal virtues and theological virtues. The four cardinal virtues are prudence, justice, fortitude and temperance. The *Catechism* emphasizes their importance among all the human virtues: "Four virtues play a pivotal role and accordingly are called 'cardinal'; all the others are grouped around them" (*CCC*, 1805).

The three theological virtues, which God gives us at our baptism, are faith, hope and charity. According to the *Catechism*, "The theological virtues are the foundation of Christian moral activity" (*CCC*, 1813).

Throughout this book we will examine these seven significant virtues and the opposing vices that are especially tempting for many women.

The more virtuous we become, the more freedom we will have. Virtues keep us from being slaves to our sin and selfishness. They enable us to become masters of living well. In striving to become virtuous women, our feminine beauty can flourish as it never has before.

Prayer

Lord God, I know that developing virtue will take effort on my part, but I also know that you want to help me. Please strengthen me with grace and be with me as I strive to cultivate virtue in my life. Amen.

Reflection Questions

1. What skills have you acquired through consistent effort?

2. Growing in the fullness of beauty includes making an honest assessment of our spiritual warts and wrinkles, so to speak. What specific vices diminish your beauty? What bad habits or habitual sins keep you from being all you were meant to be?

3. God gave you the theological virtues at baptism. How can you keep them alive in your soul?

4. Although we acknowledge our weaknesses, it's not necessary to dwell on them. Focusing on a positive plan of action for growing

in beauty is our goal. How can the virtues help you overcome your weaknesses? How can they ultimately help your true beauty to flourish?

5. Describe a woman you know who is virtuous and beautiful. How are these two qualities connected in her?

Day 3: A Super Model

For years I had a secret desire to be the most beautiful woman in the world, though I didn't realize it until I went on a pilgrimage to Fatima, Portugal.

During this trip I was asked to do a soul-searching inventory of my greatest desires. While I knew that holiness was *supposed* to be number one on my list, it wasn't. I realized that what I *really* wanted, what *really* motivated my thoughts and actions, was this incredible longing to be more attractive than any other woman on the planet. I wanted to win my lifelong battle of competing with the women who always had something I didn't: blonde hair, thin legs, white teeth, long eyelashes, small knuckles. The list went on and on.

As I pondered this reality, I actually began to question whether there even was such a thing as "the most beautiful woman." Every woman must have *some* imperfection that some other woman doesn't have, right? "Could anyone ever really deserve the title 'Most Beautiful'?" I asked myself. I happened to be sitting in the piazza in front of the Basilica of Our Lady of Fatima.

Suddenly it dawned on me that *Mary* was the most beautiful woman who ever lived. She is the subject of more paintings, sculptures, music and poetry than any other female figure in history. She has captivated people's attention for centuries longer than any glamorous movie star or gorgeous supermodel ever could.

Mary had exactly what I wanted, and it was her immaculate heart that made her so beautiful. No sin or selfishness blocked or diminished the eternal beauty of God's grace radiating through her. She was the most beautiful because she was the holiest. As the Church prays on the feast of her Immaculate Conception, "You are all beautiful, O Mary; in you there is no trace of original sin."[1]

At that moment I realized my quest for beauty would never be resolved through purely physical means. Rather I would grow in beauty as I grew in holiness. The answer to my deepest longing was, in fact, to strive to be full of grace—like Mary.

"In the light of Mary," Pope John Paul II wrote, "the Church sees in the face of women the reflection of a beauty which mirrors the loftiest sentiments of which the human heart is capable."[2] Instead of being fixated on *our* reflection in a mirror, we are called to *be* a mirror of the noblest elements of human existence! God wants women to reflect his image in a special way.

Mary reveals God's image as every woman is meant to do. She is a "super model" of authentic feminine beauty because her heart is totally dedicated to serving and loving God. In his *Letter to Women*, Pope John Paul II explained:

> *The Church sees in Mary the highest expression of the "feminine genius"* and she finds in her a source of constant inspiration ....Through obedience to the Word of God she accepted her lofty yet not easy vocation as wife and mother in the family of Nazareth. Putting herself at God's service, she also put herself at the service of others: *a service of love.*[3]

If we follow Mary's example of loving service, our "feminine genius" will be able to flourish as well. As Pope John Paul II said, "woman has a genius all her own, which is vitally essential to both society and the Church."⁴ And this specifically feminine gift is what we offer the world when we serve others with care and reverence. Indeed, the feminine genius is found in not only the "great and famous women of the past and present, but also those *ordinary* women who reveal the gift of their womanhood by placing themselves at the service of others in their everyday lives."⁵

When the angel Gabriel asked Mary to be the mother of the Savior, she replied, "I am the handmaid of the Lord" (Luke 1:38). She placed herself in a position of complete service. This response reveals Mary's willingness to let God form her life. She wanted to say yes to God's will. This openness to letting God lead makes Mary our feminine model of virtue. When we also say yes to God's action within us, he can begin to form us into the beautiful creation—the feminine work of art—that he has always intended us to be.

PRAYER

Lord God, your grace shines in Mary because of her goodness and virtue. Please fill me with the same Holy Spirit that fills her, so I can also become immaculate and beautiful through your presence within me. Amen.

REFLECTION QUESTIONS

1. Many women struggle with insecurities about their physical appearance. Have you ever felt that you were "not beautiful enough"? Explain.

2. How do you picture Mary—as a real person or as a painting or statue? What stereotypes do you struggle with, if any? How can you develop a more genuine and authentic relationship with this most beautiful of women?

3. List some reasons why Mary is a good role model for women.

4. Do you think you have the "feminine genius"? What does that term make you think of? How would you describe it to a man? How would you describe it to a little girl?

5. Think about a wife and mother whom you admire. What qualities in her stand out to you? Do you agree that her vocation is "lofty"? What does that mean to you? Do you agree that being a wife and mother is "not easy"? Why or why not?

Suggested Spiritual Activity

There's no better way to get a fresh start than by honestly acknowledging our weaknesses and resolving to do better in the future. *Consider beginning your spiritual makeover by receiving the sacrament of reconciliation.* One of the best ways to sustain the effects of your makeover would be to frequent this powerful sacrament, perhaps going once a month.

Personal Reflection and Resolution

My thoughts about this chapter:

My resolution:

chapter two

PRUDENCE

Day 4: You Need a Good Driver

During a summer vacation at an island resort, my parents decided to take a scenic horse-and-carriage ride. They boarded the elegant open-air carriage and took their places on the red leather seat. The driver snapped the reins, and the team of horses set out.

Mom and Dad sat back and relaxed as the equine quartet trotted along through the beautiful landscape. But then, with no warning at all, something went terribly awry. The driver lost control of the reins, and the four horses sprung into a wild gallop, picking up speed at a rate the delicate carriage couldn't handle.

Before my parents knew what was happening, the vehicle lost its balance, and they were thrown to the ground, directly in the path of the swirling horses. Gasping for breath, my father helped my mother to her feet, and they ran as fast as they could out of the way.

The life-threatening experience put a damper on their vacation, to say the least. It took them several days to recover from the shock. Only later did they learn that it had been the carriage driver's first day on the job! The inexperienced leadership of that driver nearly cost my parents their lives.

What a difference it would have made if the carriage had been in the hands of a seasoned driver. The energy of the team of horses could have been harnessed and skillfully directed, but instead that energy caused total chaos. Who's in charge makes all the difference.

On our journey toward spiritual beautification, our "carriage" also needs to be in good hands. Traditionally prudence has been called *auriga virtutum*, Latin for "the charioteer of the virtues." Prudence is the guiding virtue that keeps the other virtues in line. According to the *Catechism*, prudence "guides the other virtues by setting rule and measure" (*CCC*, 1806).

Saint Thomas Aquinas referred to prudence as "right reason applied to action."[1] Prudence isn't just *knowing* what's right; prudence is putting that knowledge into *practice*. The wise, prudent woman directs her actions in accord with her good judgment. And in doing so she enjoys the kind of beauty that doesn't wither with age. As Scripture tells us, "Wisdom is radiant and unfading" (Wisdom 6:12).

We should note here that the word *prudence* can carry with it a negative connotation. You may know someone who's been labeled a "prude" because of her commitment to chastity or her refusal to indulge in some illicit activity or other. We've been conditioned to think of prudence as being boring, stiff-necked and socially undesirable. Perhaps that's because popular culture rarely advocates right reason over passionate impulse. The trend is to choose the chaos of unfettered "freedom" instead of the unfading radiance of wisdom and the graceful dignity of disciplined restraint.

But in the end the chariot with the well-trained driver has the real freedom. It easily arrives at the finish line, while the wildly driven chariot crashes in the dust.

PRAYER

Lord God, please help me develop the virtue of prudence. Help me recognize when I am not acting with good judgment, and give me the grace to make better choices in those moments. Amen.

REFLECTION QUESTIONS

1. Since prudence is "right reason in action," this virtue should help you grow spiritually. How is your spiritual growth related to the choices you make? Why isn't "right reason" alone sufficient to help you advance spiritually?

2. Explain any negative connotation you have heard associated with the word *prudence*. How is the virtue different from those ideas? How is it similar?

3. Scripture relates wisdom and beauty to one another. Does this make sense to you? Do you believe that a wise woman has unfading beauty? How can a woman grow in wisdom?

4. Think of a time when you knew what was right but didn't do it. What were your thoughts at that moment? How did you try to justify your action? How did you feel after you acted against your good judgment? What can you do to make better decisions in the future?

5. Spend a moment reflecting on your daily routine. What specific choices related to relationships and responsibilities do you have to make on a regular basis? In what areas do you need to exercise more prudence? How can you begin to make the needed changes?

Day 5: Working With Wisdom

Falling in love is risky business. Passion needs prudence. Otherwise we can get swept away by emotions that cloud our judgment.

Before we got engaged my husband and I had a long-distance relationship. We missed each other so much when we were apart that it was tempting to spend all our spare time talking on the phone and all our spare money traveling back and forth to visit each other. I *felt* like abandoning my responsibilities, activities and other relationships in order to devote myself entirely to the love of my life. But, fortunately, prudence kicked in, and I didn't do anything foolish. I kept working, volunteering and nurturing my friendships because these were the wise things to do, even though my heart was being tugged in another direction.

I hadn't been so prudent in the past. After wading my way through the wreckage of a relationship gone sour, I had learned the value of this virtue and resolved to make better decisions in the future.

Through the virtue of prudence, we choose the best course of action for our specific situation. The state of being in love is only one of many situations where prudence is priceless. This virtue helps us make good choices in the midst of real, concrete circumstances. That's why we sometimes call prudence "practical wisdom."

Prudence doesn't rely on a fixed formula of behavior but rather enables us to make the best decision at any given moment. The right choice for one person in a situation may not be the same as that for another person in a similar situation. We have different callings, different jobs, different relationships and different lives. The decisions facing us vary accordingly.

Consider, for example, a single woman and a woman who is married with children. These two women are in different situations and need to make decisions based on their states in life. Suppose both were interested in making a weeklong pilgrimage to a sacred site. Prudence might decide differently for each woman, weighing the relevant factors.

For both women the pilgrimage could be a time of renewal and deepening prayer. But for the mother it would entail leaving her husband and children for an extended period of time and spending money that might be necessary for their care. Depending on her family and their situation, prudence might lead her to choose *not* to make the trip, even though such a pilgrimage is not wrong in and of itself.

Saint Catherine dei Ricci advised a friend to consider his state in life and to act accordingly:

> Religious who are separated from the world and have neither business nor family obligations are bound to lead a much more mortified and rigorous life than others. But you as the head of a great house with all the cares of a family upon your shoulders ought to be very prudent about preserving your life and health, not for the sake of enjoying this world's pleasures but in order to support your family as you should, and to give your children a true Christian training.[2]

Prudence would likewise keep a mother with children from living as though she were a nun in a cloister, for example. This essential virtue keeps us on the course we are meant to be on. It prevents us from going astray and ending up somewhere we never intended to go.

Prudence is thus a flexible virtue: It applies wherever, whenever and however it is needed. Certain things are *never* acceptable in *any* situation: They go against God's law and the truth about human nature. Prudence would never lead us to make a morally bad decision, no matter what our situation might be. On the contrary, prudence leads us to what is best. And when we face decisions that involve several options, none of which are morally evil, prudence helps us weigh those options and choose the best one.

One key to keeping on course is to let prudence take an active role in forming our conscience. We'll talk about this in the next section.

PRAYER

Lord God, sometimes it can be a struggle to manage all the demands of my state in life. Please help me accept my responsibilities and make prudent choices that are in harmony with my vocation. Amen.

REFLECTION QUESTIONS

1. Think about the duties and privileges of your current state in life: married, single or religious. What are the most important elements of your vocation? How can the virtue of prudence help you fulfill your responsibilities?

2. Have you ever struggled with exercising "practical wisdom"? What gets in the way of being practical? What distracts or challenges you?

3. Give an example of someone you know who exercised the virtue of prudence in a specific situation.

4. Why do you think Saint Catherine advised her friend to "be very prudent about preserving your life and health"? How could this advice relate to you?

5. Has an important relationship ever tempted you to act imprudently? What can you do to prevent this type of temptation?

Day 6: A Conscientious Conscience

Even though I knew next to nothing about sculpture, I could tell I was in the presence of a masterpiece. During a trip to Italy, I was viewing Michelangelo's *David* at the Accademia Gallery in Florence.

Before arriving at the magnificent rotunda where the statue stands on a massive pedestal, I passed through a hallway lined with huge chunks of stone, also on pedestals. Some of these chunks had been sculpted just enough to sprout the beginnings of a woman's head or a man's shoulder. Others were chiseled here and there, but no shape was recognizable. These stone pieces were sculptures that Michelangelo never finished.

The contrast was striking between the gleaming masterpiece, so perfect in its alignment and beauty, and those rough, amorphous blobs of rock. I could not help but marvel at the fact that the *David* once looked just as rough. The expert hand of the master sculptor had brought the dead stone to life. He released the potential inherent in the rock. He gave form to what had been formless.

Our conscience begins like a block of stone in that hallway. It has all the necessary material and the capacity to lead to something beautiful (that is, the life of virtue). Yet we have to sculpt our conscience from its simple rough form if we want it to reach its full potential.

The Church emphasizes the need to have a "well-formed conscience" (*CCC*, 1783). The cartoon image of a whispering white angel floating above one shoulder, with a pitchfork-bearing devil perched on the other, fails to illustrate what our conscience actually is: an interior guide to the truth. We are the caretakers of our conscience. We are the ones who mold and shape it to align with right reason.

Sometimes we may be tempted to use "conscience" as an excuse. We may claim that a particular sin doesn't bother our conscience. Or we may excuse ourselves from fault in a situation gone wrong because we felt we were following our conscience. The *Catechism* does teach that every person has "the right to act in conscience and in freedom" (*CCC*, 1782). But if our conscience contradicts goodness, truth, virtue and the life of faith, then that conscience is not well formed.

We have a responsibility to form our consciences well. We want our consciences to clue us in to God's will for our lives. This is where the virtue of prudence comes into play.

The *Catechism* draws an important connection between prudence and our conscience: "When he listens to his conscience, the prudent man can hear God speaking" (*CCC*, 1777). The conscience of a prudent person reveals God's voice. Prudence directs us to put in the time and effort to form our conscience well. This is the wise choice, because it means we'll be better able to hear God speaking to us. And that will help us become virtuous women.

The *Catechism* goes on to say, "It is prudence that immediately guides the judgment of conscience" (*CCC*, 1806). But how do we form our conscience in the first place, before a judgment even has to be made?

The Church teaches that we form our conscience in three ways:

1. through prayerful reflection on the Word of God
2. by contemplating the reality of the cross
3. by accepting the gifts of the Holy Spirit, guided by the teaching of the Church (see *CCC*, 1785)

These three steps are spiritual chisels that will help us sculpt our consciences. And well-formed consciences give us the freedom to shape our lives into true works of art.

PRAYER

Lord God, thank you for speaking to me through my conscience. I want to be able to hear your voice clearly and quickly, so please enlighten me as I strive to form my conscience according to your will. Amen.

REFLECTION QUESTIONS

1. Take a moment to examine your conscience. Do you see any rough spots in your life that need to be "finished"?

2. How often are you aware of your conscience? How well do you heed it? What have you done in the past to form your conscience? What can you do in the future to form it better?

3. Even though the Church proclaims the Christian faith completely and confidently, it does not teach that we can impose our beliefs on anyone. Why do you think the Church teaches that man "must not be forced to act contrary to his conscience" (*CCC*, 1782, quoting *Dignitatis Humanae*, 3, §2)?[3]

4. God speaks to us in many ways. Some people hear his voice clearly through nature; others recognize God in the people around them; still others find God most tangibly in the presence of the Blessed Sacrament; others, through reading the Bible. In what ways do you hear God's voice besides your conscience?

5. How can you incorporate the three "spiritual chisels" (prayerfully reflecting on the Word of God, contemplating the reality of the cross and accepting the gifts of the Holy Spirit guided by the teaching of the Church) into your life?

SUGGESTED SPIRITUAL ACTIVITY

Right reason assures us that we get as much out of something as we put into it. To get as much as possible out of Mass, for example, it would be prudent to put some effort into the experience by preparing ahead of time. *Consider giving some attention to the Mass readings before you go to church, so you will be better able to enter into the liturgy of the day.*

PERSONAL REFLECTION AND RESOLUTION
My thoughts about this chapter:

My resolution:

Models of Prudence

MARY

Soon after Mary gave birth to Jesus, the shepherds came to visit (see Luke 2:8–20). An angel had given them a message about the newborn Messiah, and they went to find him in the arms of Mary. When they arrived at the manger in Bethlehem, they shared with Mary the glorious words the angel had spoken to them: The Savior was born!

By this point Mary was not a stranger to angels. Gabriel had appeared to her at the Annunciation, and an angelic apparition had given direction to her husband, Joseph. Yet she did not respond hastily to the shepherds' proclamation. Instead "Mary kept all these things, pondering them in her heart" (Luke 2:19). She took time to contemplate the significance of their message and what it meant for her life.

This is a perfect example of prudence. Many new things were happening in Mary's world. There was much to take in, to evaluate and to consider. Mary prudently reflected on all of this to discern God's direction.

ABIGAIL

Abigail was the wife of Nabal, a very wealthy man who lived during the time of King David. The book of First Samuel (chapter 25) describes Abigail as an intelligent and attractive woman. She was also a prudent one: Her wisdom in a difficult situation helped save many people's lives.

Nabal, on the other hand, was a harsh and ungenerous man. When King David asked him to return a favor by providing supplies and provisions for David's men, Nabal refused. So David told his army to strap on their swords and prepare for battle.

When a servant informed Abigail about what was happening, she prudently assessed the situation. Knowing that her husband was not a man of compromise and that David's troops were about to wreak havoc on her people, she decided to appease King David with a gesture of peace. She sent him a huge load of supplies and materials for his men. Then she took the blame for her husband's actions upon herself: She asked David to forgive the transgression and forget his plans to attack.

Abigail had stepped in just in time. Her plea changed David's heart. He praised her for her prudence: "Blessed be your discretion, and blessed be you, who have kept me this day from bloodguilt" (1 Samuel 25:33).

chapter three

JUSTICE

Day 7: Making the Right Change

One afternoon when I was little, my older brother and I decided to play "store." I set up a table in my room and assembled on it stuffed animals, trinkets, games and toys. Then my brother perused the merchandise. Taking my place behind a toy cash register, I waited for him to approach the "checkout counter."

My brother finally set down the items he wanted to buy and handed me some nickels and dimes. Then he asked me for his change. I took his money, put it in my register and then took it out and handed it right back to him.

I thought I knew how this worked. I had seen Mom at the store. The cashier usually gave money *back* to Mom at the end of a transaction. My brother capitalized on my youthful ignorance about making change. He walked away with his new items *and* his money!

It didn't take long for my mother to figure out what had happened and to intervene. She explained to me what "change" was supposed to be. Then she told my brother to give back the items he had taken. He was sincerely apologetic. He knew he had taken what was rightfully mine, and that knowledge had kept him from enjoying the items he had unjustly acquired.

We both learned a lesson about justice that day, even though my mother didn't use that word to explain the situation. My brother hadn't given me my due. In exchange for the items he took, I rightfully deserved compensation. Granted, I could have freely *given* him the items as gifts, but he didn't have the right to *take* them. He repaired his act of injustice by returning the items (making reparation). And he made up for the offense against me by apologizing for what he had done (reconciliation).

Justice, according to the *Catechism*, is "the moral virtue that consists in the constant and firm will to give their due to God and neighbor" (*CCC*, 1807). The virtue of justice leads us to respect the rights of other people, not taking what is rightfully theirs nor denying them what they should rightfully have. This virtue is also concerned with how we respond to God, who deserves our love and worship, since our very existence comes from him.

Often when we hear the word *justice*, it refers to the *social* justice issues in need of attention in our world today. Many people across the globe suffer from poverty or powerlessness because of unjust social and political structures. And people suffer from injustice here in the United States, where our society tends to marginalize certain populations. Individuals and organizations striving for social justice work to change situations that virtually (or literally) enslave human beings made in the image and likeness of God. The virtue of justice calls us to do so. As Pope John Paul II wrote, "Justice will never be fully attained unless people see in the poor person, who is asking for help in order to survive, not an annoyance or a burden, but an opportunity for showing kindness and a chance for greater enrichment."[1]

We can take advantage of such "opportunities" by participating in one of the many church or community outreach programs that aim to cultivate justice in society. Many parishes sponsor initiatives that strive to bring about social justice in one form or another.

In addition to focusing on large social issues, the virtue of justice is related to our dealings with the people we encounter in our daily lives: neighbors, coworkers, family, friends and so on. God loves every person. Everyone has infinite dignity and value because he or she is made in God's image. All people deserve respect as human beings, respect for their property and possessions and respect for their basic human needs.

Respecting others' property and possessions may not be too difficult for us, and it is simple enough to respect basic human needs by supporting charitable organizations and activities. But respecting a person's right to a good reputation may be something that we struggle with on a more practical daily level. We may need to make some changes in the way we approach conversation. We'll discuss this in the next section.

PRAYER

Lord God, sometimes I am more concerned about getting my due than about giving others theirs. Please change this selfish perspective, and help me recognize any ways I can grow in the virtue of justice. Amen.

REFLECTION QUESTIONS

1. Think of a time when you acted unjustly. Were you aware of the injustice of your action? Why did you make the choice you did? How did you feel afterward?

2. Both *reparation* and *reconciliation* are necessary after we treat someone unjustly. Why do you think these two elements go together? What might happen if you made reparation without reconciling, or vice versa? How does this relate to your relationship with God?

3. It's tempting to leave issues of social justice for someone else to deal with. Problems like poverty, human trafficking and unjust

war are on such a scale that we may wonder what we could possibly do to contribute to a solution. But Christ has called us to take care of the "least of our brothers." What can you do to fight against social injustice?

4. Have you ever thought that certain people—criminals, terrorists, abusers and so on—don't deserve respect? How is that thought contrary to the Christian understanding of the human person? How would Christ have treated these people? Why does *every* human being deserve respect?

5. How can you honor the inherent dignity of the people in your life?

Day 8: Just Talking

I didn't know gossip was a sin until I was twenty-two years old. From the time I was in junior high, gossip had been a pastime for me and my friends and a way of bonding. By talking about other people, we somehow felt we were deepening our own relationships. In reality we were only leading each other further away from love and closer to selfishness.

I finally realized this after college, when I did a year of service with the National Evangelization Team (NET) Ministries. During our training we learned that harming another person's reputation was an unjust act. Right away I realized how frequently I had been involved in that. I also began to reflect on how often gossip had gone on around me. Usually these conversations didn't start out for the sake of hurting someone else but for the sake of "sharing" information. We had something interesting to talk about.

I knew it was wrong to make things up about someone (calumny), to tell lies or to reveal information I had promised not to reveal. But the thought that it could be wrong to talk about things that were true, things that had actually happened, had never crossed my mind. I didn't understand that "everyone enjoys a natural right to the honor of his name and reputation and to respect" (*CCC*, 2479). Whenever I contributed to harming a person's reputation, I was not giving that person what was rightfully due him or her.

Revealing negative things about someone when there is no *just* reason to reveal those things—even if they are true—is an offense against justice. The *Catechism* defines *detraction* as "without an objectively valid reason, [disclosing] another's faults and failings to persons who did not know them" (*CCC*, 2477). An example of "an objectively valid reason" would be aiding the prosecution of a criminal. But simply getting something off my chest, giving in to inquisitive questions from others, jealousy, boredom, anger, revenge and competition are not objectively valid reasons to harm someone's reputation.

Neither is it acceptable to reveal such information in a prayer group, under a religious guise or for supposedly sympathetic reasons. This only cloaks the detraction in what appears to be goodwill for the individual. We can seek prayers or support for people without revealing details about their situations. Just mentioning that a friend is in need of our help and prayers, is going through a rough time or is struggling with a difficult problem is plenty of information. If questions seeking more details follow these comments, we can simply decline to answer for the sake of justice and charity.

Perhaps we don't usually instigate gossip, but we may fail to do anything to stop it. When detraction begins, justice calls us to put an end to it. We can do this by changing the subject or by directly asking the gossiper to stop sharing this information. If these methods yield no results, it may be best to simply leave the area so we aren't tempted to listen or contribute.

When we respect the reputations of others, we follow Jesus'

instruction to love our neighbors as ourselves. Of course we would prefer that people not gossip about us, making our faults and failings public knowledge. Honesty requires us to admit that we too have weaknesses that we'd rather not broadcast.

Every person we encounter, regardless of his or her imperfections, has inherent dignity and value. When we practice the virtue of justice, we recognize people's true worth and respect them accordingly.

This virtue is not only about giving our neighbors their due, however. Justice also means giving God what he rightfully deserves. We will discuss this in the next section.

PRAYER

Lord God, you have always forgiven me and loved me in my most unlovable moments. Thank you for this gift. Please help me show the same compassion toward others when I face the temptation to gossip. Amen.

REFLECTION QUESTIONS

1. How does gossip offend God?
2. Has gossip about yourself ever come back to you? How did this make you feel?
3. The idea that every person has a right to a good reputation is very countercultural, as are many elements of the Christian faith. What can you do to help uphold this right for other people?
4. Have you ever found it difficult to put an end to a gossipy conversation? What makes this so hard? How could you handle such situations better?
5. What excuses have you used to justify gossip?

Day 9: Gratitude to God

Two months before our wedding, my husband and I decided to remodel his old farmhouse. The job was overwhelming: We were gutting and rebuilding the place. And we were determined to have it finished in time for our wedding day.

We did manage to get running water in the bathroom and carpet in the bedroom the day before the wedding, but there was much left to be done. We headed off on our honeymoon with the floors unfinished, the trim unpainted, the blinds unhung and furniture left to set up, to name a few of the many remaining tasks.

We arrived home a week later to a huge surprise, a finished house! Our families had worked together while we were gone to complete the load of tasks. The feeling of gratitude was immense: I felt I'd never be able to repay them for all they did. I hope you have felt this sort of overflowing gratitude at some point as well.

This is but a shadow of the massive thanksgiving we owe God every single day. How can we repay him for all he has done and all he continues to do for us? Not only has he given us life; he has also given us his love. He loved us enough to make the ultimate sacrifice, sending his Son to save us sinners who cannot save ourselves.

We have the opportunity to *respond* with love to God, who first loved us. Although we can never repay God for all he's done, we can love him in return and relate to him with generosity and thanks.

This loving response to God is part of the virtue of justice. Justice toward God is also called the "virtue of religion" (*CCC*, 1807). It is God's *due* to receive our worship. He made us; we should rightly thank and praise him for this, which is what we do when we worship him. An act of worship toward God fulfills the justice we owe him. And when we truly love him, worship is a joy, not a burden.

Private prayer as well as the public prayer of the liturgy are two of the most important ways we worship God. We may think of our daily prayer time or Sunday Mass as optional. We may only get around to them when we have time. But we practice the virtue of justice by placing the proper value on prayer, realizing that God deserves our worship.

Saint Augustine encourages us: "Try to disengage yourself from so many cares, and take a little time to think of God and to rest in Him. Enter into the secret chamber of your heart, and banish from it everything save your Creator alone and what can help you to find Him."[2]

Asking God in prayer for our needs and interceding for others is good. Such prayers of petition are one part of a healthy prayer life. They humbly acknowledge that we are dependent on God's help and that we believe he wants to help us. But prayer is more than this.

Prayer includes praising God simply for who he is, thanking him and letting him know we recognize and appreciate all he has done for us. Listening to God is another element of prayer. Part of worshiping him is allowing him to be our God, our guide and our leader. If we don't quiet down for a while every day and listen to what he wants to tell us in the silence of our hearts, we are not giving him the complete worship he deserves.

Our daily prayer time will flourish if it incorporates these three elements. An easy way to remember them is PAL—Praise, Ask, Listen. God deserves to receive these three acts of worship from us every day.

In addition to our personal prayer time, God asks us to join in public prayer with others. At Mass we have the opportunity to worship God purely for his sake, because he deserves it. He commanded us to keep the Sabbath holy, not only because this day of prayer and rest refreshes us (like good beauty sleep!) but because we owe him our worship.

Even though there are specific times and types of worship, our whole life is a chance to worship God in the ways we think, speak, act and interact. These are parts of living the virtue of justice toward God. Not only do they fulfill the rightful obligations we owe our Creator, but since he is a loving Creator, they also lead us to a happier life.

PRAYER

Lord God, you are worthy of my time and attention, my praise and thanks. With your grace, may I be able to offer you everything you deserve when I pray and attend Mass. Amen.

REFLECTION QUESTIONS

1. Reflect on a time in your life when you felt tremendous gratitude for something. What were you thankful for, and how did you thank the people involved?

2. Take a few moments to list things for which you can thank God. Think of the unique gifts and blessings that have marked the course of your life.

3. How do you feel about the idea of daily prayer time: energized, overwhelmed, fearful, confused?

4. Praise, Ask, Listen: Which of these are parts of your prayer life? Which do you need to develop?

5. Describe one of your healthiest relationships. What are the joys of that relationship? What sacrifices do you make out of love for the person? How should your relationship with God resemble that relationship? How should it be different?

SUGGESTED SPIRITUAL ACTIVITY

Part of our call as Christians is to love our neighbors as ourselves. Sometimes we may not feel this love on an emotional level, but we can always choose to do loving actions regardless of our feelings. *Consider volunteering some of your time with an organization or ministry that serves others.*

PERSONAL REFLECTION AND RESOLUTION

My thoughts about this chapter:

My resolution:

Models of Justice

MARY

Mary was a faithful Jewish woman who was the first to receive the Good News of salvation through the Messiah, Jesus Christ. Mary exemplified justice toward God in her obedience to the laws he had given to her people. She knew it was her duty to follow God's commandments. She also knew that God rightfully deserved her devotion and worship. This is why she practiced her Jewish religion piously. Indeed, Jesus was born into a Jewish home with Jewish parents, and he grew up following Jewish customs and laws.

One of the ways we see Mary demonstrating justice toward God is at the presentation of Jesus in the temple (see Luke 2:22–39). According to Jewish practice, every firstborn male child needed to be consecrated to God. Mary and Joseph traveled to the temple in Jerusalem to do so, after observing a required period of purification. There Mary presented her son, along with a sacrifice of two birds, as the Law required.

Mary knew it was only just that she offer Jesus, whom God had given her, back to his Father. She returned home after fulfilling all the prescriptions of her faith, showing justice to God through the virtue of religion.

SAINT KATHARINE DREXEL

Katharine Drexel was born into a wealthy family in Philadelphia in 1858. As she grew up she desired to serve the poor, especially African and Native Americans. Katharine began to do so by donating part of her massive inheritance to help them. But she wanted to do more.

At the age of thirty-three Katharine founded the Sisters of the Blessed Sacrament, a religious order whose mission was to serve ethnic groups suffering from social injustice. She established many mission schools around the country to serve these communities. Her order grew to include over five hundred sisters before her death in 1955.

Saint Katharine Drexel is not only a model of social justice but also a model of justice toward God through the virtue of religion. Through her worship of God, especially in the Blessed Sacrament, she found the strength to carry out her active mission of social justice. She believed that we must be in right relationship with God in order to reach out to others. "If we live the Gospel," she said, "we will be people of justice and our lives will bring the good news to the poor."[3]

chapter four

F O R T I T U D E

Day 10: A Strong Fortress

When we were kids, my brothers and I used to build forts, not out of stone or brick but out of blankets and chairs. We would suspend our mom's biggest afghan across the backs of two chairs, arranged so the blanket would reach the floor on all four sides. This created a little cave we would crawl into. From within our knitted fortress, we could safely devise strategies for combating our imaginary foes.

I loved being in one of these makeshift forts. Even though there was no real threat outside, the fort made me feel safe. It offered a confidence that inspired bravery and courage in our make-believe battles. As long as we could depend on the strength of our fort, we were ready to face any "war" that was raging outside.

In the real world a strong fort offers real security. Someone facing an attack bolsters his courage in knowing his opponents cannot penetrate the sturdy walls of his fortress. Any soldier under fire is better off with a fort than without one.

In a sense you and I are under fire too. A spiritual battle rages in our souls and in our society. The constant struggle between good and evil marks our human existence. Every day we fight with our own sinful tendencies and weaknesses. We also face a spiritual confrontation against what Pope John Paul II called "the culture of death."[1]

Sharing in Christ's victory over sin and death is not without its challenges. We need a spiritual fortress, a source of security and courage, to protect us as long as these battles continue. The virtue of fortitude provides us with this spiritual stronghold.

The Latin word *fortis* means "strong, powerful or courageous." The virtue of fortitude gives us those qualities. Fortitude provides strength to overcome our natural weaknesses and to resist temptation. It gives power to accomplish tasks we could not do on our own and to influence others to stop evil. Fortitude also gives us courage to face difficult people, events and circumstances instead of avoiding them out of fear. The martyrs overcame the fear of death through this virtue.

The *Catechism* defines fortitude as "the moral virtue that ensures firmness in difficulties and constancy in the pursuit of the good" (*CCC*, 1808). Not only does this virtue help us stay strong in the face of opposition, it also helps us be active in working for the good. This applies to us as individuals and to our role within the larger community and society. In the next section we will see how fortitude can help us in our interactions with others.

PRAYER

Lord God, when trials and temptations test my courage and strength, please help me stand firm. Help me resist any fear that would keep me from fighting against evil for the sake of your name. Amen.

REFLECTION QUESTIONS

1. How do you picture a fortress in your mind? What makes it safe and strong? How is the virtue of fortitude similar to a physical fortress?
2. The term *culture of death* suggests that there is both a preoccupation with death and a disregard for life in our society. The preoc-

cupation with death often appears through morbid music, art and fashion. The disregard for life shows up through war, injustice, disrespect, abortion, euthanasia and abuse. What specific signs of the culture of death have you observed around you?

3. All of the virtues help us grow spiritually and flourish with the fullness of beauty. Yet each virtue brings a unique highlight to our lives. What special contribution will fortitude make to your spiritual life?

4. Do stories of the martyrs inspire or intimidate you? Have you ever thought about what you would do if you had to choose between your faith and your life? Who are your favorite Christian martyrs? How did they develop fortitude?

5. What temptations, weaknesses, challenges or bad habits keep you from being "constant in the pursuit of good"? What steps can you take to overcome them?

Day 11: Facing Our Fears

During college I was surrounded by people who had vastly different morals and beliefs than I was raised with. I often felt I should speak up but, unfortunately, I never did.

When friends were swapping stories of immoral escapades over the weekend, I acted as if I were amused. When professors argued in favor of abortion, I kept silent. When classmates criticized the Church or the pope or even Christ, I nodded my head as if I understood their position.

I'm ashamed to admit that I didn't do anything to put a stop to the sacrilegious talk. I was afraid of offending somebody, causing an unpleasant argument or being considered some sort of religious fanatic.

Fear often keeps us from speaking up in situations like these. Fear can also keep us from confidently speaking the simple truth when it comes to our religious practices. For example, in certain company we might choose to hide particular facts: "I'm going to my friend's house tonight," we might declare, instead of, "I'm going to my friend's house for a Bible study tonight."

Fear can also keep us from *doing* things we ought to do, like reaching out to the socially awkward woman who has shown up at church for the first time or walking out of a movie when it's morally offensive.

This sort of fear isn't a fear for our physical life; it's a fear for our *social* life. We may be scared that being *too* Catholic, being *too* much of a witness, might alienate us from our friends, family, classmates or coworkers. We are afraid of what we might lose by speaking up or acting in accord with our inner convictions. Often we justify our lack of action by focusing on the fact that we do *know* it's wrong, as if that were enough!

Living in fearful weakness will never help us flourish as beautiful women. Rather it makes us slaves to our social vanity. It prevents us from being powerful forces for positive change in our society.

The saints and heroines of history were able to accomplish great feats because they did not cave in to the fear of what people around them would think. Often these women faced misunderstanding and rejection, but that didn't faze them. They were more interested in pleasing Christ than in pleasing anyone else. What gave them the courage to speak and act for his glory? Fortitude.

The *Catechism* tells us that "the virtue of fortitude enables one to conquer fear" (*CCC*, 1808). We might tend to think of this as a statement about something dramatic like martyrdom. After all, the martyrs conquered the fear of death through this virtue. But the chances are slim, given our place in geography and history, that we're going to face physical martyrdom. Yet fortitude is a virtue we desperately need today.

We are constantly battling fear in our daily lives. We have to deal with the fear of what it means to be a Christian: What will people think? How will we have to change if we really give our lives to Christ? Pope Benedict XVI, in the homily of his installation Mass, reflected on this reality:

> Are we not perhaps all afraid in some way? If we let Christ enter fully into our lives, if we open ourselves totally to him, are we not afraid that he might take something away from us? Are we not perhaps afraid to give up something significant, something unique, something that makes life so beautiful? Do we not then risk ending up diminished and deprived of our freedom? ... [Pope John Paul II] said: No! If we let Christ into our lives, we lose nothing, nothing, absolutely nothing of what makes life free, beautiful and great. No! Only in this friendship are the doors of life opened wide. Only in this friendship is the great potential of human existence truly revealed. Only in this friendship do we experience beauty and liberation. And so, today, with great strength and great conviction, on the basis of long personal experience of life, I say to you, dear young people: Do not be afraid of Christ! He takes nothing away, and he gives you everything. When we give ourselves to him, we receive a hundredfold in return. Yes, open, open wide the doors to Christ—and you will find true life. Amen.[2]

PRAYER

Lord God, fear for my own well-being sometimes keeps me from loving and serving you wholeheartedly. With your help I trust that I can overcome these selfish fears. Please be with me in my struggle to conquer them. Amen.

REFLECTION QUESTIONS

1. Do you recall a time when you were afraid to defend what you believed in? What was the issue at hand? How was your belief being attacked? What kept you from standing up for your belief? Would you act differently next time?

2. Think about your relationships and duties as well as your spirituality. What are some things you ought to do in these realms but sometimes fail to do out of fear?

3. What is the moral difference between knowing a decision or situation is wrong and actually doing something about it? Why is it not enough to simply acknowledge the presence of evil?

4. Make an honest assessment of how you want people to perceive you. What do you hope they will think and say about you? What perceptions would bother you most? Does your concern for making the right impression ever affect your actions more than it should? Has social vanity kept you from being completely free?

5. How can you "open the doors to Christ" in your life?

Day 12: Practicing Patience

One night shortly before I turned twenty-one, my younger brother invited me out for coffee. This was odd, considering the fact that he never drank coffee. I knew something was up.

After a little bit of small talk, my brother proceeded to gently confront me about my wavering commitment to Catholicism and the slippery moral slope I was on. He told me straight out that he was concerned about the state of my soul. I was, in fact, slowly abandoning my faith as I became more and more swept up in my vanity and desire for popularity.

At that point my brother gave me a challenge. He told me that if I left the Catholic Church without ever really giving it a chance, I would have to answer for that spiritual laziness before God. But if I spent some time reading what a Catholic should read, praying what a Catholic should pray, doing what a Catholic should do and *then* decided to leave, that would be entirely different. He then produced a fifteen-page "plan" that he had developed for me. He asked me to spend one year sincerely following it.

I agreed. The plan had me doing things like reading the New Testament and the *Catechism*, volunteering regularly, praying the rosary three times a week, going to monthly confession and attending Mass once a week. Most importantly, it had me establishing a regular prayer life on which I could actually build a relationship with Jesus.

Included in my daily prayer intentions was the grace to recognize patterns of sin in my life and the strength to resist temptation. These were two essential elements of my conversion. Not only did I have to begin seeing my sinfulness, but I also had to begin fighting against it. Fortitude was the virtue I needed for this task.

Fortitude provides more than strength, power and courage to help us overcome fear. According to the *Catechism*, fortitude also "strengthens the resolve to resist temptations and to overcome obstacles in the moral life" (*CCC*, 1808). No matter how earnestly we desire to become better women, temptations will besiege us. The saints attest to this. But fortitude helps us stay strong and resist when we are tempted to sin.

Fortitude also helps us overcome obstacles in our daily lives. Our suffering may be very difficult, like dealing with a terminal illness or the loss of a loved one. But even the small sufferings we face can test our patience. Whether big or small, suffering presents us with a choice: We can curse God and remain motionless, or we can get up and begin again with the help of fortitude.

The strength we gain from the virtue of fortitude helps us to develop the virtue of patience. Patience allows us to deal with present evils without being overtaken by them, especially evils that others inflict on us. It's not easy to be patient when we are sick, when we are accused unjustly, when we have to tolerate someone who annoys us, and so on. We need strength to control our frustration in these situations, to continue to persevere through them and to remain steadfast when dilemmas come our way. Developing patience in our daily lives helps us love the people around us and deal with situations we cannot control.

When someone has wronged us, for example, it may be all we can do to avoid being vengeful in our action and our speech. The more patient we become, however, the easier it will be to avoid not only anger but also grumbling about trying situations.

As we progress in patience, we'll move toward the culmination of this virtue: being joyful in the midst of suffering. Saint Paul demonstrated this when he rejoiced in what he suffered for the sake of Christ (see Romans 5:3). He was unjustly accused, beaten and imprisoned, but he did not lose his patience or his joy.

Such a noble response is remarkable, but it's not out of our reach. It's the fruit of the virtue of fortitude. Cultivating this virtue will help transform us into courageously patient women.

PRAYER

Lord God, when my patience is tested, I too often fail the test. Please help me to cultivate the virtue of fortitude and to call upon you when I face the temptation to complain or grumble. Amen.

REFLECTION QUESTIONS

1. Developing a prayer life requires patience. As with any relation-ship, our unity with God grows slowly over time. Do you ever have to struggle to persevere in prayer? How can you approach this without losing patience?

2. What are some of the biggest obstacles you face as you try to live a moral life?

3. Take a moment to reflect on the times of greatest suffering in your life. Did suffering ever lead you to stray from your faith or to doubt God's goodness? Did you learn anything from the expe-rience of suffering? How did it change your understanding of yourself or of God?

4. What situations or people make you lose your patience? Can you identify certain triggers that put you over the edge? What delib-erate response can you prepare in advance to help you maintain self-control?

5. Think of people you know who are joyful even when times are tough. What do you think enables them to do this? What ele-ments of their behavior could you incorporate into your life?

SUGGESTED SPIRITUAL ACTIVITY

Throughout his life Jesus faced many trials and temptations that tested his courage and resolve. *Consider reading one of the Gospels all the way through*, paying special attention to how Jesus lived out the virtue of fortitude.

PERSONAL REFLECTION AND RESOLUTION
My thoughts about this chapter:

My resolution:

Models of Fortitude

MARY

At the Annunciation the angel Gabriel told Mary, "Do not be afraid" (Luke 1:30). Part of Mary's task in accepting God's will for her life was to overcome fears about what he was asking her to do. This required the virtue of fortitude. Not only did Mary have the courage to say yes to God's request that she bear the Messiah, but she also had the courage to continue saying yes to God throughout her life.

Mary's courage was tested numerous times. At the presentation of Jesus in the temple, Simeon declared to her, "A sword will pierce through your own soul" (Luke 2:35). He was referring to the suffering Mary would endure as she shared in her son's mission. Mary did not recoil at these words but accepted them courageously.

And the tests soon began. After the Magi visited the infant Jesus, Mary had to rush off to a foreign land and hide from a bloodthirsty king in order to protect her baby (see Matthew 2:13–15).

Mary's lifelong lessons in fortitude culminated in her ultimate test at the foot of the cross. Most of Jesus' followers were not brave enough to stay with him to the end, but his mother remained at Christ's side, even at the risk of her own life.

SAINT THÉRÈSE OF LISIEUX

Saint Thérèse was born in France in 1873. She entered a Carmelite convent at fifteen years of age and spent the remainder of her twenty-four years praying for the salvation of souls. Saint Thérèse is a model of fortitude because she endured trials, both big and small, with great patience.

In her autobiography, *The Story of a Soul*, Thérèse describes how she constantly strived to show patience in bearing all things. Dealing with the small annoyances of life—a grumpy person, a drafty room, a small portion at dinner—was Thérèse's area of expertise. She knew that the virtue of patience was pleasing to God.

Saint Thérèse also displayed tremendous fortitude when she was dying of tuberculosis. This disease killed her slowly and painfully. The fact that she went through many physical tortures without anesthesia is in itself a great testament to her courage.

Thérèse had fortitude in both physical and spiritual trials, remaining courageous when spiritual temptations assailed her. She patiently persevered to the end, confident in the love of Christ.

chapter five

Temperance

Day 13: All for the Good

In the late 1800s and early 1900s, women across the United States joined together in advocating one of the cardinal virtues: temperance. These women had seen too many people, including many of their husbands and fathers, fall under the control of alcohol. As a result, their families were suffering. These women believed that drinking in controlled moderation was the solution to the problem of alcohol abuse. Hence the Temperance Movement came into being.

The movement evolved in the early twentieth century into what we now refer to simply as "Prohibition." Instead of temperance, the emphasis shifted to total abstinence from alcohol. Abstinence is necessary for alcoholics, but to expect everyone to avoid alcohol entirely was extreme.

Most of us have seen the effects of alcoholism, whether in our own families or among friends. Like any indulgence, the abuse of alcohol is due to something *good* that people are hoping to find—comfort, happiness, pleasure, peace and so on. But without temperance the good inevitably escapes them. Ultimately it's not comfortable to be a slave to alcohol, or to anything else for that matter.

The *Catechism* defines temperance as "the moral virtue that moderates the attraction of pleasures and provides balance in the use of created goods" (*CCC*, 1809). Temperance is not prohibition; It is balance, control and moderation. This virtue allows us to truly enjoy things by preventing our desire for pleasure from dominating or controlling us.

Temperance doesn't just apply to alcohol. It helps us enjoy any good thing that brings us pleasure: food, shopping, television, the Internet, talking on the phone, exercising, hobbies, work and so on. Temperance reminds us that too much of a good thing is not always a good thing. This virtue enables us to stop *before* we hit the level of "too much."

Taking this one step further, a temperate woman not only controls her *use* of good things but also directs her *desires* toward what is good. She uses discretion in what she allows herself to desire. With conscious effort (at least in the beginning), she chooses to channel her inclinations in a positive direction.

Temperance trains us to sincerely desire the things that are truly good for us. With the help of this virtue, we can form our hearts to long for the truth, goodness and beauty that ultimately come from God.

PRAYER

Lord God, help me recognize the things that I am too attached to and dependent upon. My desire is to depend on you alone. Please give me the grace to rely on you instead of worldly comforts. Amen.

REFLECTION QUESTIONS

1. In what areas do you have the most difficulty practicing self-control? Have you ever deliberately worked on exercising more control in those areas? If so, did you make progress or hit a wall?

2. Through the virtue of temperance, we can shape and direct our desires in a positive way. For example, when I practice enough self-control to cut back on sweets, I lose the urge to eat them and

start enjoying healthier foods at the same time. When my will leads, my desires follow. Has temperance given you new freedom in some area?

3. Where do you find help when you are tempted to overindulge?

4. How could you help a friend or family member who struggles with temperance? What kind of support assists without judging or criticizing?

5. Meditate on the public ministry of Christ. How did he practice temperance?

Day 14: Choosing Chastity

I worked for a few years on the "preventive" side of the pro-life movement: chastity education. It always made sense to me that if our culture would embrace the true meaning of sex as a lifelong, life-giving bond of love between a husband and wife, abortion rates would decrease dramatically. If single people saved sex for marriage and married people stayed faithful to their spouses, many "unwanted" pregnancies would never happen in the first place.

Part of my job at that time was sharing this message with students. Looks of confusion usually appeared on their faces when I told them that *everyone* is called to chastity, even married people. Chastity is much bigger than abstinence: It's respecting God's plan for sexual intimacy. This respect happens in different ways for single people, those in religious life and married people.

Chastity is a matter of recognizing the sacredness of sexual union. For those who are not married, including priests and religious, respecting sex does mean practicing abstinence. Those who are chaste in marriage speak the language of love when and with whom God intends them to speak it, namely, their spouse!

Respecting the gift of sexuality brings authentic freedom to men and women, regardless of their state in life. It liberates them from the emotional pain, social turmoil, physical risks and spiritual suicide of sex outside of marriage. And chastity is a virtue everyone can embrace, even those who have not chosen it in the past.

Chastity is God's invitation to happiness and true love. But chastity doesn't stand alone. It comes hand in hand with the virtue of temperance. The *Catechism* tells us that temperance "ensures the will's mastery over instincts" (*CCC*, 1809). The sexual drive is instinctual within us, and temperance helps us master that drive instead of letting it master us. Our human sexuality is more than just a physical urge: It's a built-in call to make a complete gift of our very self to another person. Temperance allows us to offer this beautiful self-gift freely and generously, if and when the time is right.

Chastity helps single people and those in religious life resist temptations to be sexually active. And it enables married people to resist temptations to be unfaithful to their spouses.

An insightful definition of chastity comes from *The Truth and Meaning of Human Sexuality* by the Pontifical Council for the Family: *"Chastity is the spiritual power which frees love from selfishness and aggression."*[1] The document focuses on the importance of self-mastery, emphasizing that before we can *give* ourselves, we have to *possess* ourselves.

Chastity is a *spiritual power*. It is a strength that goes beyond our bodies, beyond what is physical. God wants us to have this supernatural strength. He also wants to help us form the virtue of temperance to make us all the more powerful in practicing chastity.

Chastity *frees love*. It frees love from selfishness, aggressiveness and possessiveness. Through the virtue of temperance, we can embrace chastity and experience love as it is meant to be.

Love cultivates temperance and chooses chastity because going against chastity *always* puts the other person at risk, emotionally, physically, socially and spiritually. Real love, on the other hand, goes out of its way to protect the beloved from harm. Chastity lets this love flourish.

PRAYER

Lord God, you know that today's culture does not encourage chastity, and I know that you are calling me to practice chastity nonetheless. Please give me temperance in my moments of weakness, so I can master myself and choose real love. Amen.

REFLECTION QUESTIONS

1. Think about the relationship between unchastity and abortion. How would you explain this connection to a skeptical friend? What ideas and choices could you practice and promote to help reduce the number of abortions in your community?

2. What are the benefits of following God's plan for sexual intimacy?

3. How have the media, your peers and perhaps your own experiences shaped your thoughts and feelings about sex? Do you feel that you received the best formation possible on this important topic? What ideas do you need to redirect or purify in order to acknowledge sexual intimacy as a complete gift of self?

4. What are your strongest instincts and drives? How can temperance help you master these instincts?

5. How can you preserve your commitment to chastity?

Day 15: Curbing Cravings

"Just do it." "Obey your thirst." "Go with the flow."

Our culture doesn't exactly proclaim the message of temperance. Focusing on self-control and restrained balance doesn't seem to be an effective marketing tool. Most of the messages we pick up encourage impulsive, passion-driven behavior without any discussion of limits or boundaries.

I was dismayed when I glanced at the label of a shirt in the juniors' section of a department store. The brand name was "No Boundaries." What are we trying to communicate here? That boundaries are no good? That it's stylish to go to extremes?

Real freedom requires self-control. If I'm not in control, if I'm always "obeying my thirst," then I'm going to be a slave to that thirst. Doesn't it make more sense to obey God, our omnipotent, omniscient Father who loves us unconditionally and wants to make us eternally happy, who gives commands only to set us free? Why would I choose to be a slave to something as powerless as my own cravings or instincts? Why would I want to be a slave to *anything* for that matter?

Temperance frees us; self-control liberates us. We can use our free will to shape our lives into something beautiful.

Yes, we do have drives and instincts, but so do squirrels. What they *don't* have that we do (among other things) is the capacity to practice temperance. These walnut-craving beasties—and all the other animals—simply cannot exercise the freedom that leads to moral excellence and eternal bliss.

Scripture references the virtue of temperance, even if that exact word isn't used. It often speaks in terms of food and drink, but the concept can apply to anything we desire or crave. Think of this passage from Sirach as an encouragement to practice chastity, for example:

> Test your soul while you live;
>> see what is bad for it and do not give it that.

For not everything is good for every one.

...

Do not have an insatiable appetite for any luxury,
     and do not give yourself up to food;
for overeating brings sickness,
     and gluttony leads to nausea.
Many have died of gluttony,
     but he who is careful to avoid it prolongs his life.
(Sirach 37:27–31).

Giving in to our "thirst"—whether it's for more clothes than we can fit in our closet, for yet another piece of chocolate, for a constant stream of social engagements or for sexual intimacy with someone we're not married to—doesn't make us more beautiful women. It makes us prisoners of our cravings.

Because things can be so attractive at the moment of temptation, temperance is a tremendous tool to have at our disposal. It enables us to calmly and easily say, "No, thank you. Not right now." The woman who can say these words at the right moment is protecting both her freedom and her beauty.

PRAYER

Lord God, with your help I can be free of any kind of slavery to my superficial desires. But I know I can't do it on my own power. Be with me when I need to say no. Amen.

REFLECTION QUESTIONS

1. Have you ever indulged in something after seeing a commercial or advertisement? Was that a good choice? How can you practice self-control when watching TV commercials or looking through magazines?

2. Think of a time when you successfully exercised self-control.

What was the situation? Why did you choose temperance? How did you feel after conquering the temptation to give in?

3. Do you agree that obeying God's commandments brings true freedom? Why or why not?

4. What things do you have an "appetite" for besides food? What can you do to grow in temperance regarding these things?

5. The virtue of temperance helps us live an orderly life, to stay on task instead of giving in to the distractions of the moment. Keeping the house clean, sticking to a schedule for work or school and managing time well all relate to self-control. How would you rate yourself on a scale of 1 to 10 when it comes to keeping order in your life? What could you do to move closer to 10?

SUGGESTED SPIRITUAL ACTIVITY

Perhaps the most tried and true method of growing in temperance is the practice of fasting. *Consider giving up one treasured food or activity for a period of time* as a way of growing in self-control. You can also offer the sacrifice as a prayer for a special intention.

PERSONAL REFLECTION AND RESOLUTION

My thoughts about this chapter:

My resolution:

Models of Temperance

MARY

Mary spent her whole life in perpetual dedication to God. She is a model of purity. Any temptation that arose against chastity never got any further than that. Mary was in control of herself, not a slave to pleasures or whims.

In addition to chastity, Mary showed temperance regarding other earthly pleasures. At her son's birth three wealthy wise men visited her (see Matthew 2:1–12). These were important and influential men. Most likely they arrived not only with gold, frankincense and myrrh but with a caravan of servants, animals and supplies. Mary could have taken advantage of the situation. She could have taken something for herself, capitalizing on the wealth of her visitors and the importance of her son. But materialism didn't hold power over Mary. She was devoted to God, not to costly possessions or the power of human connections.

Mary also could have sought rewards during Jesus' public ministry. She could have demanded special attention from those who followed her son or used his influence to indulge in her own comfort and glory. But Mary wasn't like that. The virtue of temperance kept her from placing too much importance on worldly prestige or pleasure.

SAINT AGNES

Agnes lived in Rome during the early fourth century. She was a beautiful young girl, both inside and out. Agnes loved Jesus and was dedicated to living her life entirely devoted to him. She is a model of temperance because she didn't give in to the temptation to gain pleasure at the cost of her soul.

Agnes's beauty and virtue attracted the attention of the governor's son, who was not a Christian. He was intent on having Agnes for himself, and he tried to win her over through various gifts, bribes and promises. Agnes could have married this wealthy and prominent man and had a life of comfort and ease. But she was totally dedicated to Christ and did not let the attraction of these things rule her.

Agnes's self-control in resisting these temptations infuriated the governor's son. He told his father that Agnes was a Christian, a crime punishable by death. The governor then attempted to sway Agnes's resolve by offering her rewards for revoking her faith. But the virtue of temperance kept her from placing too much value on these perishable rewards.

Next the governor tried to destroy Agnes's commitment to chastity by sending her to live with women of ill repute. But this did not shake her virtue. Agnes stayed true to her faith. She was martyred at the age of thirteen.

chapter six

Day 16: Give and Take

Almost every time I compliment something of my mother's, she tries to give it to me.

"That candle smells nice, Mom."

"Oh, thanks. Here, you can take it for your kitchen."

Or, "I love that skirt, Mom."

"Thanks, I got it on sale. Here, it would look nice on you."

It's quite an interesting phenomenon. Maybe it comes with the selflessness of being a good parent, or maybe it's just my mom, but the fact remains that she's incredibly generous.

Whenever this happens I'm faced with a choice. My mother is giving me a gift with no hidden motives, only love. She offers her possessions to me with complete freedom, no strings attached. The candle, the skirt or whatever, could be mine.

But I always ask myself, what should I do with this gift? Should I take my mom's nice thing and walk out the door, feeling justified because she gave it to me? Or should I "return" the gift to Mom, with as much generosity and love as she showed me? (Most of the time, since I love her too and appreciate the sacrifices she made to acquire the item, I "give" it right back to her, touched that she loved me enough to offer it to me.)

We can ask ourselves a similar question about our lives. We did not bring ourselves into existence. Our very being is dependent on God, who gave us life through his generosity and love. He cares about each of us infinitely more than anyone could ever care about a candle or a skirt or anything else. So we have a choice to make. Will we freely give the gift of ourselves back to God, or will we cling to the life that is now ours?

The virtue of faith enables us to return the gift of our lives to the loving hands of the Giver. As the *Catechism* tells us, "By faith, 'man freely commits his entire self to God'" (*CCC*, 1814, quoting *Dei Verbum*, 5).[1] We don't have to commit ourselves to God; we are free to commit ourselves to a thousand other things. But faith helps us love God and respond appropriately to the love he showed by bringing us into being. When we return the gift of ourselves to God, he responds with even more generosity: He gives us the gift of knowing him more intimately through divine revelation and the Church.

"Faith is the theological virtue by which we believe in God and believe all that he has said and revealed to us, and that Holy Church proposes for our belief, because he is truth itself" (*CCC*, 1814). This is the formal definition of faith in the *Catechism*. God gives us this theological virtue at our baptism. But it's up to us to cultivate the seed of faith planted in our soul.

Giving ourselves back to God means placing our trust in him. Faith allows us to humbly acknowledge that we are not our own creator but that God exists, that he created us and that his providence is at work in our lives. Faith also helps us accept the words and signs God revealed in Sacred Scripture and Sacred Tradition to help us know him. The magisterium of the Church—the pope teaching in union with the bishops—helps us interpret and understand this revelation. Through faith we accept the guidance God gives us in his Church. We receive all these blessings when we give our lives back to God.

Once we have freely committed ourselves to God through faith, we can discern and do God's will. Instead of following our own will or striving to possess our lives apart from God, we will look to him and embrace his loving plan for our lives. Filled with the joy of knowing and accepting God, we will naturally want to share this joy with those around us.

PRAYER

Lord God, you made me and gave me so many blessings. Thank you for all the gifts you have bestowed upon me. I want to live my life in gratitude for your goodness and generosity. Please help me be grateful. Amen.

REFLECTION QUESTIONS

1. What do you think is the real purpose of gift giving?
2. Some people struggle to see their life as a gift. A painful childhood, an experience of abuse, illness or tragedy can make life feel miserable. How would you try to convince someone that life is a gift from God?
3. Can you identify a particular moment when you made a decision to return the gift of your life to God? Have you waffled on this offering? Where do you stand right now in regard to giving your whole life to God?
4. Have you experienced clarity in knowing God's will for you? Have you ever experienced doubt or uncertainty? How do you discern major decisions in your life?
5. How can Sacred Scripture, Sacred Tradition and the magisterium help you live Christianity to the full?

Day 17: Good News

"So how did he propose?!?"

We always want to know the details. Each story is unique. I've heard of a romantic proposal on a park bench, a diamond ring strategically placed on a mountaintop and one that showed up in an Easter egg, a beautiful photo scrapbook whose last page read, "Will you marry me?" and a hot-air balloon ride that lifted off with a dating couple and landed with an engaged one.

I enjoy hearing these tales and sharing the excitement of the people I love. But I've never been as excited as the day I got to tell my own story.

My husband-to-be thought of every detail to show me how much he loved me, beginning with an early morning proposal at the adoration chapel (where we were applauded by the grinning elderly couple sitting in the back). Next he took me on a road trip, with my favorite Elvis songs playing in the background. At our destination we climbed a church tower just in time to hear all the bells ringing as we gazed out over the glorious landscape. Our day culminated in a trip to an art museum and an exquisite Italian dinner.

Now, whenever someone doubts that men and women are inherently different, I can tell them what happened when we arrived at my grandmother's house that evening. As soon as we walked in, my parents, aunts and uncles congratulated us. Then, within a matter of minutes, all of the men, *including my new fiancé*, sat down in front of the television to focus on the rest of the Packers' game. The women, on the other hand, formed a circle—completely oblivious to the fact that we were directly in front of the TV—giving me hugs, laughing, asking questions and expressing little outbursts of pure glee. When we noticed the men craning their necks to see around us, we got the hint and moved the party upstairs.

For the men the announcement was made, and then life went on as usual. But the women knew this was the biggest day of my life thus far, and we wanted to *talk* about it, to *communicate*, to *relate* with one another.

This is concrete evidence that women are naturally relational beings. And it makes sense. Didn't God create Eve (that is, woman) to fulfill the human need for *relationship?* Adam was a solitary being until she showed up. One of her gifts to the world was specifically *to be in relationship.* This helps explain why women love to share good news about engagements or anything else; it goes along with our relational nature and our social inclinations.

So why should it be any different with the good news of the gospel? We women have a gift for communicating and sharing. If we truly believe the gospel—if we have the virtue of faith—then shouldn't we be sharing the news with the people around us? God loves us! Christ saved us! All people have the offer of eternal peace and joy if only they accept it. Why do we so often tend to keep this news to ourselves?

Here's a summary of the Good News:

1. God made us.
2. He loves us.
3. We have separated ourselves from him through sin.
4. He sent his Son Jesus to die on the cross to save us from our sin and reconcile us to himself.
5. Jesus rose from the dead and ascended into heaven, where we hope to one day join him.

This famous verse also summarizes the gospel: "For God so loved the world that he gave his only-begotten Son, that whoever believes in him should not perish but have eternal life" (John 3:16). We can live in unending happiness and love if we want to. Jesus paid the price through his death to cancel the debt of our sins. Our salvation is his free gift to us.

We cannot earn this gift, but we can either accept it or reject it. If we've truly accepted it in faith, then we will want others to know the freedom of accepting the gift too. Our faith isn't meant to be hidden inside our own hearts and minds. Faith is meant to spread out beyond us to the whole world.

The *Catechism* tells us that "The disciple of Christ must not only keep the faith and live on it, but also profess it, confidently bear witness to it, and spread it" (*CCC*, 1816). One of our great strengths as women is speaking and communicating with others. We are being Christ's disciples when we use this natural strength to speak openly about our faith, about its joys and rewards and, more importantly, about how much God loves us.

Why hesitate to speak about the Good News whenever we can? When it's not appropriate to speak directly about our faith, we can still bear witness through a life of virtue in which we consistently act in accord with our faith. As the saying goes, "Preach the gospel at all times, and when necessary use words."

PRAYER

Lord God, you are calling me to share the gospel. But sometimes my feelings get in the way, feelings of being unworthy or overwhelmed or uninterested. Please remove these obstacles so that I can share the good news of your love with others. Amen.

REFLECTION QUESTIONS

1. Can you think of a time when you have seen evidence of women's relational nature? Do you agree that women have a special gift for relationships?

2. When you reflect on the basic gospel message, what part of it touches you most deeply? Why do you think that part stands out to you?

3. Think of the times in your life when you have had the opportunity to share your faith with others. Have you always taken advantage of the opportunity? Have you ever been hesitant to speak with others about your faith?

4. What can you to do profess, bear witness to and spread the faith? How can you preach the gospel without using words?

5. How would you explain to a non-Christian the fundamental Christian truth that Jesus reveals God's love to us?

Day 18: Fearless Friendship

Girls can be cruel. I think I'm still recovering from the social wounds I incurred during junior high and still feeling guilty for the ones I inflicted on others. The cliques at the lunch table, the brutal rejections on the playground, the snobbish criticisms about what people were wearing or how they looked. Alas, I was not the exception to the rule; we all did this to one another.

In this toxic social environment, our only form of defense was to form a sort of contract with one other girl who was designated "best friend" and with whom there was an unspoken agreement not to abandon one another. It was almost like an exchange of services. Whether you had anything in common with one another or really got along was insignificant. The result was a strange possessiveness in these exclusive relationships, which were based more on fear than on friendship.

Unfortunately, this is how some people view their relationship with Jesus. They stay Christian more out of fear than out of faith. They understand Christ as their Savior but not really as their friend. His role is little more than a form of insurance against hell. This is a tragic reduction of who Jesus wants to be in our lives.

When we think of Jesus as merely someone who offers us the "service" of salvation, we miss out on the beauty of a real friendship with him. And when there's no real relationship, there's no chance we're going to be good witnesses to the faith. Instead of introducing Jesus to the people we know, as we would do with any real friend, we often just keep him to ourselves.

Keeping our faith to ourselves is easier if we just think of it as a set of beliefs or a philosophical system we have chosen to live by. But Christianity is not about a *what*; Christianity is about a *who*. A Christian has committed himself or herself to a lifelong, loving friendship with Jesus. As with any real friendship, certain beliefs and behaviors accompany it.

Some of us do have a solid friendship with Jesus but are still afraid of imposing on people by sharing our faith and introducing them to him. This fear keeps others from hearing the Good News. It also keeps them from hearing the invitation to a life of salvation, joy and freedom. If we care about the people around us, why would we withhold such a priceless invitation?

Saint Josemaría Escrivá wrote, "There are also souls who, whether they know it or not, are looking for Christ and have not found him. But 'How can they hear about him, if nobody tells them?'."[2]

The antireligious forces in our society want us to believe that faith should only be private and personal, that sharing our faith with others is offensive, intolerant and disrespectful. But if we know Jesus, if we are really exercising the virtue of faith, we will be less likely to fall for these misguided ideas. Jesus offers love and salvation. It's a mistake to believe that such an offer could be disrespectful. If we forced someone to accept the offer, that would be a problem. But to give a friend an invitation to something marvelous is actually a sign of *respect* for that person.

So what's to stop us from introducing Jesus to the people we know? As women we are naturally relational. We tend to care about people and friendships, but sometimes we care about them in a disordered way. We can become so concerned about whether someone approves of us, or about keeping a certain friend, that we might not be willing to leave our comfort zone in the relationship. In our modern culture sharing Jesus with others usually requires us to rattle the status quo. So we are afraid.

But Scripture tells us that "perfect love casts out fear" (1 John 4:18), and Jesus came to set us free. The virtue of faith offers us the chance to break out of the chains of fear. Again, Saint Josemaría Escrivá tells us, "let us say quite fearlessly: Dearest Jesus, we are working for you."[3]

Prayer

Lord God, I want to know you personally. I want to be connected to you and energized by our relationship. Please reveal yourself to me so my faith, and my desire to share my faith with others, will be strengthened. Amen.

Reflection Questions

1. How would you describe your relationship with Jesus? Do you feel content with the relationship as it is? How could it grow deeper?

2. Were you raised Christian, or are you a convert to the faith? In either case, why have you chosen to follow Christ? How would you explain your choice to a nonbeliever?

3. Can you recall a time when you have experienced resistance or hostility from others because of your beliefs? How did it make

you feel? Did it strengthen or weaken your faith?

4. Do you have any fears that keep you from doing something out of the ordinary for the sake of sharing your faith? Does concern for social approval sometimes prevent you from revealing your true self—faith and all? How can you work to overcome these fears?

5. Think about the qualities you would describe as feminine. How could these unique gifts help you spread the faith? What can you do to cultivate these traits?

SUGGESTED SPIRITUAL ACTIVITY

The traditional hymn used during Benediction of the Blessed Sacrament urges us, "What the senses fail to fathom, / Let us grasp through faith's consent."[4] Believing in the presence of Jesus in the Eucharist—Body, Blood, soul and divinity—is a great act of faith based on Christ's words and actions. *Consider spending time in adoration of the Blessed Sacrament on a regular basis.*

PERSONAL REFLECTION AND RESOLUTION

My thoughts about this chapter:

My resolution:

Models of Faith

MARY

Through the virtue of faith, we believe in God's promises, trusting that what he tells us is true. Mary is a perfect model of the virtue of faith, because once God revealed his plan to her, she didn't doubt. The angel Gabriel explained that Mary would conceive by the power of the Holy Spirit and bear a son. And she believed it.

It would have been easy to believe this once she began to feel the effects of her miraculous pregnancy. But Mary believed even before her body began to give clear, concrete evidence to confirm the angel's words. She believed, purely out of faith, that a miraculous pregnancy had occurred in her body. She trusted that the Incarnation had happened, even though she only had God's word to go on.

Mary demonstrated faith in this reality when she went to visit her cousin Elizabeth. The Gospel of Luke (1:39–56) records how Mary "went with haste" to share the Good News and to carry the presence of the living God to her kinswoman. What a tremendous act of faith for Mary, just recently impregnated by the Holy Spirit! Elizabeth, filled with the Holy Spirit, realized the greatness of Mary's virtue and cried out, "Blessed is she who believed that there would be a fulfilment of what was spoken to her from the Lord" (Luke 1:45).

SAINTS PERPETUA AND FELICITY

These women lived at the beginning of the third century in Rome, a time and place of fierce Christian persecution. Perpetua was a well-educated noblewoman and mother of a young son. Felicity, a slave, was eight months pregnant when she and Perpetua were imprisoned for being Christians. Both women are models of faith because they gave their whole lives to God and were not afraid to be witnesses to the gospel.

Perpetua was twenty-two years old when she told her father she had become a Christian. He was angry with her decision and begged her to give up this new faith. But she didn't waver, even after her father attacked her and threw her in prison. There she developed a friendship with Felicity, also a convert to Christianity.

The two women prayed together and set an example of faith for the soldiers and guards. Even on their last day, as they were thrown into the Colosseum with wild beasts, they urged the crowds who were mocking them to accept Christ. In her last moments Perpetua uttered these words, which so perfectly match her actions: "Continue firm in the faith, love one another, and be not scandalized at our sufferings."[5]

chapter seven

HOPE

Day 19: Promises and Prayers

Have people ever made promises to you that they didn't keep? Most of us have experienced this a few times. We've placed our trust in people who didn't live up to their claims.

If you've gone through this, you know how devastating it can be. We expect people to follow through on their word, even though we, too, may be guilty of breaking promises. My mother used to warn me to "beware of pie-crust promises that are easily made and easily broken." People can be flaky and fickle at times. We are not perfect, and neither are our promises.

God's promises, on the other hand, are perfect. They are trustworthy because he is trustworthy. We give credence to our own promises by associating them with him ("I swear to God...").

God, our loving Father, has told us that he loves us and that he sent his Son to save us. He has promised eternal happiness with him in heaven. At times we might be tempted to doubt this promise. But the supernatural virtue of hope helps us believe in God's power to save us.

Hope as a theological virtue is more than just a whimsical wish for a particular outcome. It is the proper perspective about God's promise of salvation. The *Catechism* defines hope as "the theological virtue by which we desire the kingdom of heaven and eternal life as our happiness, placing our trust in Christ's promises and relying not on our own strength, but on the help of the grace of the Holy Spirit" (*CCC*, 1817). The virtue of hope helps us overcome natural human doubts and rest in the confidence of God's promises, not because of anything *we* have done but because of *his* power.

God has promised that salvation is available to us. But just because he promised doesn't mean we will automatically take him up on the offer. How do we secure our hope in this promise? By our faith in Jesus Christ.

Faith and hope work together. Saint Paul refers to "Christ in you, the hope of glory" (Colossians 1:27). Jesus is our hope. Keeping our eyes fixed on him sustains us, even in difficult moments.

But how do we keep this constant focus on Jesus? The *Catechism* tells us that "Hope is expressed and nourished in prayer" (*CCC*, 1820). We meet Jesus in prayer. If his presence in us is our hope of glory, we will want to invite him to take up residence in our souls.

Saint Teresa of Avila emphasized the importance of prayer in preparing our souls to receive Jesus. She referred to prayer as "frequent solitary conversation with [Jesus] who, as we know, loves us."[1] Prayer is time spent with our friend Jesus. His loving presence within us, nourished through this sort of prayer, fills us with hope, which leads to abiding joy.

PRAYER

Lord God, my hope wanes when I distance myself from you. I want to be connected to you every day, and I know that prayer is essential for this connection. Please inspire me with the desire to converse with you in prayer. Amen.

REFLECTION QUESTIONS

1. Think of a time when you had an experience of broken trust. How did it affect your ability to trust again? What about a time when you were guilty of breaking someone else's trust: How did you work to regain it?

2. When things don't go our way, we sometimes blame God, as if he let us down somehow. But in truth God is always looking out for our best interests. Do you believe that God is completely trustworthy? How would you defend this idea to people who felt God was against them?

3. How does God's promise of salvation affect your everyday life? Do you think about it regularly? Do you thank God for it? How do you handle your relationships and responsibilities in light of this promise?

4. Has there been a time in your life when you lost sight of Jesus? Why did that happen? What were the results? How can you keep your focus on him in the future?

5. Think about your experience of prayer. Do you think of it as a conversation with Jesus? How would you define prayer?

Day 20: A Joyful Side Effect

I was a grumpy bride-to-be. It's not that I didn't want to get married or that I didn't love my fiancé; it was just that the task of planning a wedding completely overwhelmed me. The whole process of picking out flowers and dresses and a reception hall and a photographer and a cake and table favors and everything else was supposed to be a girl's dream come true. But as the date of our wedding rapidly approached and we still had *so much* to do, I began feeling hopeless and anything but joyful. I was afraid that the day would end in disaster, that our guests would be miserable and that my husband and I would begin our married life in utter humiliation and despair.

My fiancé, on the other hand, was completely calm and unruffled. I couldn't understand how he was able to smile throughout this whole ordeal. "Just trust in God, Gina," he kept encouraging me. "Everything's going to work out fine." I got upset at him for being so darn hopeful without any tangible *evidence* for hope.

Of course, as it turned out, the wedding was beautiful, and the reception was a big hit with our family and friends. And I learned a valuable lesson from my faithful fiancé: The virtue of hope isn't about *knowing* that I've got a perfect plan to work everything out; it is about *trusting* that God is bigger than our problems, and he's got everything under control.

For all the time I spent preparing my hair, my nails, my makeup and my body in the days leading up to our wedding, my sour moods spoiled my appearance on more than one occasion. I missed a golden opportunity to grow in the virtue of hope and in authentic beauty.

Times like these make me realize that I am in serious need of a spiritual makeover. I'm inspired by the saints, who faced much more severe trials than wedding planning and handled them well, thanks to the virtues they worked hard to cultivate. Take Blessed Teresa of Calcutta, for example.

Even before her death, many people referred to Mother Teresa as a saint. We know how generous she was. We know how influential, prayerful and holy she was. And we know too that she was loving and joyful throughout her whole life. Only recently, however, have we learned about the deep struggles that afflicted her soul for fifty years.

After her death several of Mother Teresa's letters were published, revealing the private workings of her soul. In these letters she described feelings of darkness and isolation from God. She suffered tremendously on the inside as she went through these spiritual trials. But most people had no idea she was suffering so deeply because she exuded joy. "My smile is a great mantle which covers a multitude of sufferings," she wrote to her spiritual director.[2]

Mother Teresa preserved her joy because she never lost her hope. Even in her painful interior trials, she continued to trust in God. The *Catechism* tells us that hope "keeps man from discouragement; it sustains him during times of abandonment" (*CCC*, 1818).

Most people feel abandoned or discouraged at some point in their lives. Life brings difficulties. We suffer tragedies. But one of the great side effects of the virtue of hope is that even in the midst of our trials, we can have joy. We can smile and mean it. We can be cheerful as we continue on our way.

Mother Teresa knew that being joyful was not necessarily easy all the time. Yet she was always smiling and encouraging others to do the same, even when it was a challenge:

> It is easy to smile at people outside your own home.... It is difficult to be thoughtful and kind and to smile and be loving to your own in the house day after day, especially when we are tired and in a bad temper or bad mood. We all have these moments and that is the time that Christ comes to us in a distressing disguise.[3]

Joy itself can be hard work. But nonetheless we can nurture it in our hearts. The theological virtue of hope is the key to seeing this joy blossom and grow within us.

We can share the gift of joy with those around us. As daughters, mothers, sisters, wives, friends, classmates and coworkers, we can impact other people. By choosing joy, not only do we benefit but the people we love do too.

Women who radiate joy are especially beautiful. Strengthening our hope helps this feminine beauty flourish.

As Christians we can depend on the hope of Christ at all times. Through him we know that "hope does not disappoint us" (Romans 5:5).

PRAYER

Lord God, there are times when I fail to radiate joy. I give in to my own pain, sorrow or fear instead of trusting in you. Please strengthen the virtue of hope in my soul, so I can smile even in the midst of these trials. Amen.

REFLECTION QUESTIONS

1. Do you agree that joyful women are especially beautiful? What do you think it is about joy that corresponds to beauty?

2. Thinking back on a struggle you have faced or a time when you felt overwhelmed, can you identify a situation that actually helped strengthen your hope? How can hope grow in the midst of trials?

3. Were you aware of the fact that Mother Teresa suffered such difficult spiritual trials? Have you ever had experiences of feeling separated from God? How did you cope with that sense of spiritual darkness?

4. What are some areas in your life where you need to make a decision to be joyful?

5. What are your greatest hopes? How do you think the supernatural virtue of hope relates to those desires and dreams?

Day 21: Staying in Balance

One of my favorite playground toys was the seesaw (or teeter-totter, depending on your geographic region). I always loved bouncing up and down while carrying on a playful conversation with a simultaneously bouncing friend.

For a seesaw to work, however, there has to be balance. If I was too much heavier than my friend, there wouldn't be any movement. My friend would just hang suspended in the air while my end dragged to the ground.

Imagine that the virtue of hope is located at the center of the seesaw. At the high end of the plank, imagine my friend holding a sign that says "presumption." On the end that's stuck in the dirt, imagine me holding a sign saying "despair." Despair and presumption result when we knock hope off balance.

Presumption happens when a person becomes too self-assured. Presumption takes something for granted: It assumes; it demands. A person may *presume* that she will automatically go to heaven because God promised we could go there, but she has lost sight of the fact that we *accept* this promise by accepting Jesus. And we can reject Jesus through serious sin.

A woman who is presumptuous may think that just "being a good person" in a general and vague sense will automatically get her into heaven. She thinks the deal is already sealed. Hope, on the other hand, trusts that God will follow through on his commitments while realistically acknowledging that we have a part to play as well.

Despair happens when hope gets off balance in the other direction, sinking down into darkness and fear. Despair is the complete loss of hope. Instead of presuming that God *has* to save me, despair fears that God *cannot* save me, no matter what he does. Someone in the state of despair feels she is too far gone, that her sins are too great for God to forgive. In effect, she believes that God is not all-powerful. She mistakenly thinks that even if he wanted to, he would not be able to keep his promises in her case.

Despair afflicts many women in our society. Women who are suffering through a divorce, women who battle drug or alcohol addictions, women who bear the scars of adultery or unchastity, post-abortive women and many others often struggle with feeling unforgivable. Victims of abuse also deal with feelings of despair: The virtue of hope is sometimes suffocating in their souls (even though they were not actually at fault) because they find it so hard to release the pain they have carried for years and to trust anyone again, even God.

Being trapped in either despair or presumption is like being on a seesaw that can't move. It's a paralysis of the soul. Hope unlocks the hinge, allowing our souls to have the free, joyful, carefree spirit of a trusting child.

God gave each of us the gift of hope at our baptism. Our task is simply to accept the gift and incorporate it into our lives.

PRAYER

Lord God, you know the dark places in my soul. You know where I need your light to heal me and change my despair into authentic hope. I give you permission to enter these hidden places and to transform them by your grace. Amen.

REFLECTION QUESTIONS

1. How would you explain the supernatural virtue of hope to someone of a different religion? How would you explain its effects on a person's life? Can you give personal testimony of how this virtue has affected your life?

2. Do you struggle with either presumption or despair? Which one are you more inclined toward? Why?

3. What can you do to nurture the virtue of hope in your life?

4. Can you think of a person you know who is in need of true hope? What is preventing this person from being hopeful? How can you help?

5. Describe how you have seen hope and joy expressed in young children. What can you learn from them?

SUGGESTED SPIRITUAL ACTIVITY

Our faith teaches that everyone is called to holiness; we are all called to be saints. We should never lose hope that this is actually possible for us. Rather, we should rely on God's grace and exert our best efforts. *Consider reading chapters four and five of the Vatican II document Lumen Gentium,* on the laity and the universal call to holiness.

PERSONAL REFLECTION AND RESOLUTION

My thoughts about this chapter:

My resolution:

Models of Hope

MARY

The ascension of Jesus into heaven must have left his followers with a bittersweet feeling. They had witnessed the miracle of the Resurrection and knew that Jesus had power over death. But now they had to say good-bye to him again. They must have wondered what would happen next, when he would return, whether they would really see him in heaven.

Mary also faced the question of whether or not her son would fulfill his promises. She chose to hope that he would.

Mary had suffered with her son during his passion; she had rejoiced in his victory when he rose from the dead. And now, as he took his place in heaven at the right hand of his Father, she hoped that he would indeed send his Spirit to lead and guide his followers until he came again in glory.

We know that Mary hoped in this promise because she continued to pray after Jesus had ascended into heaven. The Acts of the Apostles tells us that Mary was with those who gathered together in the Upper Room. They were all devoted to prayer (see Acts 1:14). The prayer Mary offered testifies to her hope that Jesus would fulfill his promises.

HANNAH

In the First Book of Samuel, we read about Hannah. She was married to Elkanah, but they did not have any children. This was a great source of pain for Hannah. She is a model of hope because she prayed and trusted in God's power even in the midst of her pain.

At first though, Hannah struggled with despair. She was the subject of ridicule year after year because she had no children. Perhaps feeling as if she was at the breaking point, she took her sorrow and hopelessness before the Lord in prayer. She poured out her worries and her desires to the Lord, asking him to bless her with a son.

Through this heartfelt prayer Hannah received the hope that comes from God alone. She returned to her regular activities and was no longer downcast.

Not only did Hannah receive the hope that is nourished in prayer, but she also saw the fulfillment of her hope: She conceived and bore a son, Samuel. For this great gift she proclaimed a beautiful prayer of thanks to God (see 1 Samuel 2:1–10). She rejoiced that he had heard her prayers, recognizing that his power, not her own, had satisfied the deepest desire of her heart.

CHARITER

CHARITY

chapter eight

Day 22: Virtue Glue

About a year ago I decided to host a Christmas party for some friends. I wanted to plan an evening of creative yuletide festivity, so among other things, I decided to make sugarplums.

Now, I had no idea what sugarplums actually were. I had only heard about these sweet delights in Christmas poetry. So I got out *Christmas Cooking for Dummies* and learned all about them. Along with a few drops of rum, each plum was to contain a mixture of coconut, dried fruit and nuts.

But when I tried to shape the mixture into little balls, the pieces of fruit and coconut refused to adhere. I didn't have time to figure out what was wrong, so I ended up serving the "sugarplums" as a heap of disordered bits and pieces, which my guests had to eat with spoons. It wasn't until later that I realized I had left out the key ingredient: rum!

While dried fruit, nuts and coconut have their charm, the overall effect was lost because there was no adhesive to give form and flavor to the sugarplums. There was no bonding agent to create unity. Something very important was lacking.

As we work to develop virtue, we might face a similar situation if we're not careful. Developing a heap of isolated good habits that we toss together randomly isn't the ultimate goal. We want to join these virtues into a unified whole that gives form and flavor to our femininity. So we need a bonding agent.

According to Catholic tradition, charity (love) works as excellent virtue glue. Saint Paul instructs us, "And over all these put on love, which binds everything together in perfect harmony" (Colossians 3:14).

The *Catechism of the Catholic Church* defines charity as "the theological virtue by which we love God above all things for his own sake, and our neighbor as ourselves for the love of God" (*CCC*, 1822). If we love God more than anything else, and our neighbor as ourselves, then our lives will be properly ordered. This order in our soul, resulting from true charity, enables the other virtues to flourish.

On the other hand, if we lack charity, then our beauty remains incomplete, because any other virtues we may have are missing their full value. Saint Paul describes this idea:

> If I speak in the tongues of men and of angels, but have not love, I am a noisy gong or a clanging cymbal. And if I have prophetic powers, and understand all mysteries and all knowledge, and if I have all faith, so as to remove mountains, but have not love, I am nothing. If I give away all I have, and if I deliver my body to be burned, but have not love, I gain nothing. (1 Corinthians 13:1–3)

Through our baptism, in which God gave us the supernatural gift of charity, we have the *ability* to love him above all else and to love others. But that doesn't mean we have always *exercised* that ability. If sin or selfishness obstructs our love, we need reconciliation.

God generously offers us his forgiveness through the sacrament of reconciliation. Regularly approaching the Lord through this humbling and healing sacrament is like a trip to the spiritual spa. It is one of the best "treatments" available for our spiritual beauty.

PRAYER

Lord God, I know that charity is the most important virtue. Please fill my soul with true charity, so I can love you with my whole heart and love those around me as well. Amen.

REFLECTION QUESTIONS

1. We use the word *love* more often than the word *charity*. What do you think of when you hear each word? How are those ideas connected to the virtue of charity?

2. Saint Catherine of Siena wrote in her *Dialogue*, "Every perfection and every virtue proceeds from charity."[1] Why do you think the other virtues need charity in order to flourish? Why is charity so important?

3. Think about some ways you have put charity into action. Can you identify any patterns? Do you tend to practice charity in a particular way? How could you expand the way you live out this virtue?

4. What is your experience of the sacrament of reconciliation? Do you take advantage of this sacrament on a regular basis? How can it help you strengthen your charity?

5. How is loving your neighbors a reflection of your love for God? Have you always thought of it that way? Have you ever felt God's love for you through the charity someone else showed to you?

Day 23: A Friendly Fruit

I reserve the term *close friend* for those women with whom I feel a deep, lasting, personal connection. These relationships are blessings God gives me not only to help me enjoy life but to grow spiritually as well.

Of course I share common interests and experiences with these wonderful women, but those alone are not enough to make our friendships thrive. These relationships remain rooted because of our mutual commitment to God and to one another. We make efforts to be in regular contact with each other. We sacrifice time and energy to listen to each other and support each other when times are tough. We also affirm one another, because we recognize and appreciate the beauty we see in one another. These friendships have enriched my life.

True friendships like these are fruits of charity. God intended friendship to be a reflection of his love for us. He loves us so generously and unselfishly that he came into our world as a powerless infant to share the common experience of human life with us. Taking his unselfishness further, he made painful sacrifices to restore our friendship with him when we rejected it through sin.

God didn't *need* to do any of this. His love for us is not necessary for his existence. He has freely chosen to make these offers of friendship because of the love that overflows from his heart.

When we nurture true friendships, we have a chance to do something similar. We have the chance to cherish people out of love, not out of need. The love of friendship is a special kind of love precisely because it is not strictly necessary.

C.S. Lewis talks about friendship in his book *The Four Loves:*

> Friendship is—in a sense not at all derogatory to it—the least natural of loves; the least instinctive, organic, biological, gregarious and necessary. It has least commerce with our nerves,... nothing that quickens the pulse or turns you red and pale.... [W]e can live and breed without Friendship.[2]

This doesn't mean we *should* live without friendship. Lewis's point simply reminds us that we *could*, just as God could live without us.

But he didn't want to. Similarly, if we have charity in our hearts, we won't want to live without friendship.

Friendship not only makes life more enjoyable; it also reveals God's image to the world. When we love a friend without seeking our own interests, we reflect God's love. The more people we treat as friends, the more we are putting charity into practice. Every person we encounter—every neighbor, coworker, acquaintance and relative—offers us a chance to love as God loves. He said to Catherine of Siena, "This is why I have put you among your neighbors: so that you can do for them what you cannot do for me—that is, love them without any concern for thanks and without looking for any profit for yourself. And whatever you do for them I will consider done for me."[3]

Because women tend to be socially oriented, enjoying relationships and time with people, we possess a natural tendency toward the beautiful gift of friendship. In effect we have a head start on this fruit of charity because of our in-built desire to become involved in the lives of those around us.

Sometimes, however, we allow our relationships to fall out of the realm of charity. In the next section we will discuss how to prevent this from happening.

PRAYER
Lord God, help me to value friendships as a way to practice charity. Help me to honor my friends and to be open to making new ones. Help me unselfishly give to my friends and receive your love through them. Amen.

REFLECTION QUESTIONS
1. Think about your closest friendships, especially the ones you've had for the longest time. Based on your experience, what are some characteristics and benefits of true friendship?

2. How do you think friendship reflects the kind of love God has for us? How can a good friendship help a person feel valuable?

3. Have you always thought of Jesus' love for you as an offer of friendship? If so, what made you think that way? If not, what prevented you from thinking in those terms?

4. Do you agree that women have a natural gift for relationships? Why do you think God would have given women this special gift?

5. Can you think of a time when you made friends with someone you weren't initially attracted to? What got you past your first impression? How can you cultivate friendships with a wide variety of people?

Day 24: The Forbidden Fruit

We all know the story of Adam and Eve in the Garden of Eden. You could probably tell the whole tale from start to finish right now. I think you'll know what I mean when I summarize it like this: Paradise, one rule, a snake, an apple, shame.

Adam and Eve lived in a perfect world: no worries, no trauma, a great relationship with God, each other and creation. They had the whole garden at their disposal except for one tree. God only made a single guideline for them to follow, which was for their benefit. But when the serpent tempted them to doubt and to disobey God, they gave in to the temptation. Then they hid themselves out of guilt (see Genesis 3:1–8).

This story should sound familiar, not just because we've heard it before but because we have experienced it ourselves. We don't always choose virtue. The inclination that attracts us toward sin is what the Church refers to as "concupiscence." It's a consequence of living in a sin-infected, "fallen" world. When we face temptation we often go a step further by actually giving in to that temptation, even though we know we are going against God's will.

So the situation of Adam and Eve is not an irrelevant myth that has nothing to do with us. On the contrary, it ingeniously describes each of us every time we commit a sin.

Most of us can recall times when we've let our selfishness and pride rule the day. We've also sometimes misused gifts for our own personal designs. Take the gift of friendship, for example.

Sadly, we don't always base our relationships on true charity. Sometimes we form social alliances for our own benefit, seeking the pleasure, popularity or promotion that a "friendship" might win for us. Using another person is never a fruit of charity. Those of us who have been used know how unloved we felt on realizing it. No one wants to be treated as an object. Such use stands in stark contrast to true love.

We can abuse the gift of friendship in other ways. Instead of reaching out to reconcile a broken relationship (as Christ has done for us), we might allow anger to fester and to tempt us to slander a former friend. Or we can be hypocritical in our so-called friendships, being sweet and charming one minute and turning our back to gossip, accuse and criticize the next. Unfortunately, these scenarios are not uncommon among women. Our natural tendencies toward people and relationships become ugly and distorted when charity ceases to be the guiding force behind them.

Slander, gossip, backbiting, jealous competition, hypocrisy and cliques all destroy the friendship, companionship, support and encouragement God calls us to give and receive through charity. But if we exercise this beautiful virtue, we can foster healthy relationships that bring authentic joy and peace.

PRAYER

Lord God, help me avoid spoiling friendships through my own sinfulness. Please teach me to be generous and compassionate, forgiving and kind, as you have always been with me. Amen.

REFLECTION QUESTIONS

1. As you reflect on the story of Adam and Eve, what elements of their situation ring familiar? Do you identify specifically with a certain part of their experience? What strikes you as most foreign?

2. How would you explain concupiscence to someone who had never heard the word? What concrete evidence can you give to suggest that we do have this disordered attraction to sin?

3. Have you ever been used in a relationship? How did that make you feel? Have you ever used someone else to get something you wanted? What effect did that selfish motive have on the life of the relationship?

4. Saint Paul's Letter to the Galatians lists the fruits of the Spirit: "love, joy, peace, patience, kindness, goodness, faithfulness, gentleness, self-control" (5:22–23). How can these fruits of the Spirit help you resist sin? How can you plant these fruits in your soul?

5. Why do you think people form cliques? What are they seeking to gain by excluding others? What do you think Jesus would say to them about this behavior?

SUGGESTED SPIRITUAL ACTIVITY

The more we reflect on all Christ did out of love for us, the easier it will be for us to love him wholeheartedly in return. Meditating on his life, death and resurrection can help us grow in charity. *Consider praying a daily rosary, paying special attention to the mysteries for the day.*

PERSONAL REFLECTION AND RESOLUTION

My thoughts about this chapter:

My resolution:

Models of Charity

MARY

Throughout this book we have seen that Mary exemplifies the virtues beautifully. She didn't just have one or two of them, she had them all. She had an ample supply of "virtue glue": charity. She was first and foremost a woman of charity, so all the other virtues could flourish in her as well.

Her charity is evident throughout her life but especially at the moment of the Annunciation. There Mary made a perfect act of love by freely offering herself as God's handmaid. She gave the gift of herself and her life back to God, whom she loved above all things.

Mary is sometimes called "the New Eve" because she put God first, exactly what the original Eve failed to do. Mary didn't view her act of self-giving as a restrictive burden but rather as a joy, because she acted out of love. Her self-surrender was followed by the great love song known as the Magnificat: "My soul magnifies the Lord, / and my spirit rejoices in God my Savior" (Luke 1:46–47).

Because of the great love in Mary's heart, she never acted contrary to charity. This virtue filled her soul and prepared fertile ground for the other virtues to grow. All of Mary's virtues flowed from her loving response to God's will. His grace—the same grace that is available to us through prayer and the sacraments—filled her from the first moment of her existence.

SAINT GIANNA BERETTA MOLLA

Gianna lived in Italy from 1922 to 1962. She was a wife, a mother of four and a doctor. Taking a special interest in helping mothers, babies, the elderly and those in poverty, Gianna saw her medical practice as mission work. She is a model of charity because she embodied Christ's words, "Greater love has no man than this, that a man lay down his life for his friends" (John 15:13).

Gianna laid down her life for her daughter, just as Christ laid down his life for all of us. When she was pregnant with her fourth child, her doctors found an ovarian cyst that was causing major complications in the pregnancy. She could have aborted the baby in order to save her own life, but Gianna would not do anything that threatened her child.

Gianna's daughter, Gianna Emanuela, was born April 21, 1962. Saint Gianna died seven days later. This heroic act of charity crowned Saint Gianna's lifetime witness of service and love to those around her.

chapter nine

VIRTUE VERSUS VICE

Day 25: Ugly as Sin

Women in the United States spend an average of six billion dollars a year on makeup alone. Since the late nineties expensive "beauty" procedures such as liposuction and breast augmentation have increased by over 100 percent. Many women are willing to exchange their hard-earned money for the chance to be more physically attractive, according to worldly standards, anyway.

Women don't want to become uglier. Imagine how shocked we would be if a beautiful woman paid for plastic surgery in order to deform her shapely nose. How would we react if a woman with a perfect complexion rubbed grease over her face every morning in order to stimulate acne? What if a woman with long, dark eyelashes took a pair of scissors and cut them off? These actions would strike us as totally bizarre.

When we hear stories of saints who marred their appearance in the name of modesty or chastity, for example, we recoil and wonder why. It's important to remember that these women are not saints because of their extreme actions; they are saints because of their great love for God. Even such holy women didn't do everything right. It is, in fact, unreasonable and inexplicable for a woman to deliberately destroy her God-given beauty.

Yet how often do we disfigure our souls through sin? Vice overshadows the soul's natural goodness and beauty. The dark cloud of selfishness extinguishes the light of charity, turning a bright soul into a black hole.

As Christians we are called to be the light of the world, but sin keeps us from shining with our full radiance. Saint Paul instructs us:

> for once you were darkness, but now you are light in the Lord; walk as children of light (for the fruit of light is found in all that is good and right and true), and try to learn what is pleasing to the Lord. Take no part in the unfruitful works of darkness, but instead expose them. (Ephesians 5:8–11)

Just as we would not deliberately do something to deform our appearance, we should not deliberately do anything that would extinguish the light in our souls. Maybe if we remember this analogy between physical beauty and spiritual beauty, we will be less inclined to give in to temptations to sin.

The *Catechism* defines sin as "an offense against reason, truth, and right conscience" (*CCC*, 1849). We can easily see that destroying physical beauty doesn't make sense; the Church teaches us that sin doesn't make sense either: It offends reason. Why would we do something that makes us spiritually ugly? Why would we turn away from a God who loves us, who knows how to make us happy and who is the original source of all true beauty in the world?

Such unreasonable behavior happens when we give in to our selfishness. Just as virtue becomes easier with practice, so does vice. One lie leads to another. One unchaste act leads to another. We become desensitized to the gravity of our sin as we get more and more used to it. What we once knew was clearly wrong, dangerous or disordered can begin to seem justifiable after we have given in to it.

The *Catechism* tells us: "Sin creates a proclivity to sin; it engenders vice by repetition of the same acts. This results in perverse inclinations which cloud conscience and corrupt the concrete judgment of good and evil. Thus sin tends to reproduce itself and reinforce itself" (*CCC*, 1865).

Vice is vicious. Not only does it cloud our good judgment, but it also stifles our capacity to love. The *Catechism* states: "Sin sets itself against God's love for us and turns our hearts away from it" (*CCC*, 1850). God's love is constant. Only *our* response is subject to change. Either we respond according to our nature and bear God's beautiful image to the world, or we reject our connection to God and act as if we don't need him.

How truly blessed we are that, even when we reject God, disfiguring our souls through sin, he still loves us. He welcomes us back when we sincerely repent. The sacrifice of Christ on the cross saved us when his blood was "poured out for many for the forgiveness of sins" (Matthew 26:28).

Tradition identifies seven capital or "deadly" sins, which lie at the root of many other sins. The *Catechism* lists them as "pride, avarice, envy, wrath, lust, gluttony, and sloth" (*CCC*, 1866). Virtue is the antidote to these vices. Particular virtues counteract each of these sins. We will examine the seven deadly sins and the virtues that overcome them in the next sections.

PRAYER

Lord God, help me keep my soul beautiful. Because I cannot see my soul or feel it, I often forget about it. Please help me remember every day the value of my soul. Amen.

REFLECTION QUESTIONS

1. Take a mental inventory of all the beauty supplies you own. About how much money do you spend a month on makeup, trips to the salon and related items? How much time do you spend shopping for or using these things? Why do you think American women in general spend so much on beauty tools and strategies?

2. What elements of your physical appearance do you feel good about? What elements do you struggle to accept? How about your spiritual "appearance"? What are your spiritual strengths and weaknesses?

3. Have you ever thought of sin as making you ugly? How can sin negatively affect your external appearance?

4. Is there a period of your life that you would describe as being shrouded in the darkness of sin? What led you out?

5. Do you agree that both virtue and vice become easier with practice? If so, why do you think this is the case? If not, why not?

Day 26: A Virtuous Defense

The rear bumper of my first car was tied to the body of the vehicle with a hefty piece of yellow twine. A friend of mine had rear-ended me shortly after I got my license, and the rope was my dad's temporary solution to the resulting problem. Being a self-conscious junior in high school at the time, I was mortified every morning when I had to drive my already embarrassing old boat of a car to school; the ridiculous rope only made matters worse.

Although I cringed whenever people saw me get in or out of this gigantic machine with its sagging bumper, the twine taught me a valuable lesson: I could likely have avoided the problem (and ultimately the twine) if I had been more attentive to what was going on around me while I drove.

Learning the techniques of operating a vehicle and the meaning of the signs and signals on the street does no good if I fail to get out of the way when a drunk driver swerves in my direction (or when my friend is following me too closely). I need to be a *defensive* driver. I have to be ready for an "attack" at all times. If I'm not on the lookout, I could easily be caught in an accident.

The same is true in our spiritual life. Learning how to cultivate and develop virtue is not enough. If we desire the safety of our souls, we need to be on the lookout for any threats to our spiritual safety, vigilantly defending ourselves against these dangers. Consciously developing certain virtues can help us ward off the threats posed by the seven deadly sins.

Consider avarice, otherwise known as greed. This vice lurks everywhere. Television commercials, billboards, magazine advertisements and Internet pop-ups lure us to want more and more: more clothes, more cosmetics, more housewares, more money, more amusement, more success. It's as though we can never have enough.

This vice leads to dissatisfaction and discontent. It can also lead to sins of injustice toward our neighbor if we seek gain without taking other people's rights into consideration.

The best way to defend against an attack of greed is to develop the virtue of generosity. Greed cannot take root where generosity has already been sown. The virtue of generosity flows from the virtue of charity (see *CCC*, 1829). To love is to be generous instead of selfish or possessive.

A generous woman is not only willing to share but actually wants to do so. She has no need to hoard things for herself but is happy to share with others. The virtue of generosity protects a woman from getting caught in the tailspin that results from an endless quest for more.

Next, consider gluttony. Again, this vice is easy to "feed" in our culture. Super-sized portions, all-you-can-eat buffets and bottomless bowls of food tempt us. We have such easy access to snacks and quick meals that we can shovel food into our mouths without really being conscious of what or how much we're consuming.

Some of us also have a tendency to eat "comfort" food to deal with our emotions, leading us to eat to excess.

A woman of temperance, however, will have a ready shield to defend her when gluttony makes a move. If she is well versed in self-control, then culinary indulgence won't get the best of her. She will be able to enjoy food without becoming a slave to her appetite. She will be able to eat reasonable portions instead of feeling compelled to consume more and more.

This same virtue of temperance is a powerful defense against the deadly sin of lust. Modesty and chastity, which flow from temperance, destroy lust's power. When the vice of lust tempts us to use another person—whether physically or mentally—for our own selfish gratification, the virtue of chastity will be prepared for the attack.

It's not that a chaste person is never *tempted* to lust. Rather, the virtue of chastity enables a person to resist *giving in* to that temptation. This virtue enables us to stop short of sexual sin, suffocating the vice before it takes hold of our soul. And be assured, lust can easily take root in our sex-saturated culture.

Modesty fights lust from another angle: It actually helps reduce the *temptation* toward lust. A modest woman refuses to present herself as an object of lust for men. By respecting herself, dressing and acting in a manner consistent with her dignity, she makes it easier for others to respect her. A modest woman does her culture a great service.

But modesty also requires temperance in our fashion-conscious world: It requires the self-control to resist all the latest fads. This is not to suggest that modesty is incompatible with fashion. Some of the most stylish and attractive outfits are perfectly modest. It may just take the virtue of hope to persevere in finding them!

Greed, gluttony and lust stem from what the *Catechism* calls "a perverse attachment to certain goods" (*CCC*, 1849). Possessions, amusements, food and sexual intimacy are not bad; they are "goods" that God gives us, along with the responsibility to use them well and in an ordered way. Sin happens when our *attachment* to these things becomes disordered. As we will see in the next section, sin can also result when we are overly attached to ourselves.

PRAYER

Lord God, please teach me to recognize and defend against the attacks of greed, gluttony and lust. Help me squelch any temptations these vices present by being prepared in advance with virtue. Amen.

REFLECTION QUESTIONS

1. We do many things to protect our physical beauty: We exercise, try to eat healthy foods, practice good hygiene and grooming and so on. What do you do to protect your spiritual beauty? Is there anything you need to add to your routine to have a good defense against spiritual decay?

2. Our culture doesn't tend to see gluttony as a sin. If anything, gluttony is only seen as a risk to our physical health. How would you explain the spiritual risks of gluttony?

3. Do you struggle most with greed, gluttony or lust? What can you do to overcome temptations in these areas?

4. Think of a woman you know who is very generous. How has she practiced this virtue? Have you ever benefited from her generosity? What can you do to grow in this virtue?

5. How would our society be different if modesty were a cultural value? What are some ways you can cultivate modesty for yourself? For other women in your life?

Day 27: The Victory of Virtue

Imagine if Jesus would have succumbed to the vice of sloth. How different would human history be if he had been too lazy to go out and preach? What if he had decided not to work any miracles because he just couldn't find the motivation? Imagine Jesus giving up during a journey to a neighboring town because he didn't feel like walking anymore. The Good News would have gone nowhere.

Or what if Jesus had been jealous of the apostles? What if he had refused to send them out two by two because he was afraid they would get more followers than him? Suppose he had chosen not to give them the power to bind and loose sins because he wanted that power all for himself. How different would human history be if Jesus had deliberately stifled the effectiveness of the apostles out of pure envy?

Jesus did get angry. We know he showed *righteous* anger at the cleansing of the temple and when confronting the foolishness of the scribes and Pharisees. But the deadly sin of anger (or wrath) is not righteous. It is rooted in hatred and violence, not in justice.

Imagine if Jesus got angry every time things didn't go his way, when people resisted his preaching or made too many demands of him. Imagine if Jesus had cast the first stone at the woman caught in adultery because he was mad at her for sinning. If Jesus had given in to anger instead of showing love and mercy toward those around him, he would not have been practicing what he preached. He certainly would not have attracted many followers.

Finally, suppose Jesus had given in to the sin of pride. Suppose he refused to experience the humility of being born as a man in the first place. Suppose he refused to be obedient to God the Father by taking up the cross and dying for our sins, an act of perfect humble obedience. If Jesus had been prideful, our salvation would not have happened.

Of course, this is ridiculous imagining. Jesus is "the image of the invisible God" (Colossians 1:15), and he did everything out of love. But my point is to show how detrimental vices can be to the spread of the gospel, to the life of the Church, and how virtue makes all the difference.

In each sinful scenario I imagined, Jesus would have been thinking only of himself as opposed to anyone else, including his Father in heaven. Saint Augustine once described sin as "love of oneself even to contempt of God" (*CCC*, 1850, quoting *The City of God*, 14, 28). The *Catechism* further tells us, "In this proud self-exaltation, sin is diametrically opposed to the obedience of Jesus, which achieves our salvation" (*CCC*, 1850). As Christians we are called to imitate the obedience of Jesus and to strive to be free of destructive vices.

Just imagine the difference between our lives with these sins and our lives without them. How effective could we be in spreading the gospel if our laziness didn't hinder us? How much love could we share with others if we were never envious of them? Imagine the healing power of not giving in to anger. And imagine how powerfully God could use each one of us if we were only humble enough to let him be in charge!

If we don't want these deadly sins to threaten our spiritual beauty, we need to prepare our defense ahead of time with a bountiful supply of virtue. Specifically, we defend against sloth by cultivating the virtue of perseverance, which springs from both fortitude and hope. We need strength and courage to push through tasks that overwhelm us. And hope helps us maintain motivation by enabling us to trust that it's worth forging ahead.

As for envy and anger, these vices cannot take hold of a heart already full of charity. Charity wards off anger by enabling us to be gentle and kind, even when someone offends us. This is a reflection of God's burning charity, his infinite love for us, revealed in his mercy when we offend him through sin.

Through charity we also desire what is best for others. Envy is a failure in charity because it leads us to resent another person for what she possesses. It tends to go beyond wanting her beauty, her success, her talent or her nice house to the point of wishing that she *didn't* have those things.

Gratitude also defeats envy. Gratitude springs from the virtue of justice, which recognizes that we already have gifts we didn't earn by our own power. God gave us life and salvation. This deserves gratitude, not grumbling about what we may not have been given.

Justice helps us fight pride as well. Through the virtue of justice toward God, we recognize that he is our maker. We are dependent upon him. This realization leads to the virtue of humility, the antidote to pride.

Faith also helps us stifle prideful tendencies by enabling us to believe in a good and loving God who wants what's best for us. Pride cannot convince us to act as if we were gods when we have faith in the one true God.

PRAYER

Lord God, I want to be virtuous, but I know I have to fight against my selfish tendencies. Please be my constant companion as I strive to cultivate virtue and root out vice. Amen.

REFLECTION QUESTIONS

1. Of the seven deadly sins, which ones have you struggled with the most? How would your life be different if you had never given in to these sins? What can this teach you for the future?

2. How is sloth encouraged today in ways that it wasn't encouraged in your grandparents' generation? What objects, ideas and services promote laziness in our modern culture? How do these things affect you?

3. What makes you jealous of others? Identify any trends and ask yourself: What are the root desires that lead me to envy? What can I do to purify these desires? How can I plant charity in their place?

4. Does the virtue of humility appeal to you? What opportunities do you have to grow in this virtue? Do you welcome them?

5. What can you thank God for *today*?

SUGGESTED SPIRITUAL ACTIVITY

The Second Vatican Council referred to the celebration of the Eucharist as "the source and summit of the Christian life."[1] In the quest to live a life of virtue, receiving the Eucharist gives us grace to be the Christians we are called to be. *Consider attending a weekday Mass at least once a week.*

PERSONAL REFLECTION AND RESOLUTION

My thoughts about this chapter:

My resolution:

Models of Repentance

SAINT TERESA OF AVILA

Teresa of Avila, who lived in sixteenth-century Spain, became not only a saint and doctor of the Church but also a great mystic who was advanced in the ways of contemplative prayer. But she didn't start out that way.

Although Teresa entered the Carmelite Order when she was twenty years of age, she didn't experience a true conversion for another thirteen years. As Teresa reveals in her autobiography, she was full of pride. She was overly concerned about her appearance and always wanted to be the center of attention. God had given her the social gifts of being charming, witty and beautiful, and she gloried in these things for herself instead of humbly thanking God and using her gifts for his honor.

Teresa also struggled with the sin of gossip, even in the convent. She used to sit in the guest parlor chatting with friends and often, giving into gossip.

One day a powerful experience changed Teresa. She was praying in front of a sculpture of the wounded Christ, when she suddenly felt tremendous sorrow for all that he had suffered for her. For the first time she realized the ingratitude behind her sins, and she resolved to battle them with the help of God's grace. And so began her lifelong mission of transforming her soul into a suitable home for her eternal King.

SAINT MARGARET OF CORTONA

Although Margaret lived in the late thirteenth century, elements of her story will sound familiar to many women today. When she was nine years old, her father married a woman who was harsh and cold toward her. As she moved into her teens, Margaret began to hunger for the affection missing in her life. Unfortunately, she sought it in the wrong place.

When a wealthy cavalier from a neighboring Italian town started paying attention to her, Margaret fell for his promises of love, riches and marriage. She left her home to live with him as his mistress. But he never committed himself to her, even though they had a son together.

Margaret reveled in a life of luxury, sexual indulgence and vanity. She would parade proudly about the city in the latest fashions, giving no heed to the sin and scandal that marked her life—until the day she found her lover murdered in the forest.

For the first time Margaret felt the pangs of conscience. She wondered about the state of her lover's soul and her own. She returned to her father's home seeking forgiveness, but her stepmother rejected her. So with her son she sought the help of a Franciscan priest. His guidance assisted Margaret in her resolution to practice chastity and embrace her faith. She chose a life of simplicity, dedicating herself to the service of the poor and sick.

VIRTUOUS WOMANHOOD

chapter ten

Day 28: A Papal Surprise

During my late teens I began thinking it was my duty as a woman to criticize the Catholic Church. Although I had been raised Catholic and gone to Catholic schools, certain people had strongly influenced me to interpret the Church's unwavering opposition to abortion as an offense against women's "reproductive rights." And the constant Catholic teaching that contraception distorts God's plan for sexual unity and that sex is meant for marriage seemed ancient and irrelevant, a ridiculous roadblock to the advance of women's liberation.

Similarly the priesthood seemed to be nothing more than a structure of oppression. The fact that women couldn't be priests, well, *that* was the ultimate offense. How dare the Church suggest that men can do something that women can't!

It was while I was of this mind-set that my younger brother sat me down with the plan I mentioned earlier. One of the assignments for my year was to read Pope John Paul II's apostolic letter *On the Dignity and Vocation of Women*. By the grace of God I actually read it. And I couldn't believe my eyes.

Here was the pope—the leader of this supposedly woman-hating organization—telling me that I had inherent value *as a woman*, that I was actually *equal in dignity* to men and that I had gifts that the world desperately needs. And not only that, this pope was actually

100

acknowledging and apologizing for the way women have suffered through the centuries! He clearly argued that this oppression is the result of the very sin that Christ came to conquer, a mission the Catholic Church now carries on.

My world turned upside down—or should I say right side up? I began wondering if the Church, rather than being the *cause* of all our problems, might actually be the solution we were looking for. I wanted to learn more. I wanted to understand *why*, in light of the sentiments the pope expressed, the Church still upheld the all-male priesthood and its teachings on sexual morality.

I decided to study theology. And much to my surprise, I learned that there were answers, very *good* answers, to all of my questions.

A fundamental concept I found both liberating and exhilarating was that of the complementarity of men and women. This idea is rooted in Scripture. In Genesis 1:27 we first learn about it: "So God created man in his own image, in the image of God he created him; male and female he created them."

This passage reveals that God made *all* of humanity in his image. So since men *and* women bear God's likeness, they both enjoy an undeniable, irrevocable dignity. But there is nonetheless a distinction between them. God chose to reveal his image through two different but complementary forms: the masculine and the feminine.

The image of God on earth would be incomplete without both males and females. Men reveal something unique about God, and so do women. Taken together, we get the divine image, the whole picture, so to speak. Apart we don't. This is what complementarity is all about.

As we seek to grow in the fullness of feminine beauty, it helps to remember that God gave us special gifts and inclinations that reflect particular aspects of who he is. One of the gifts that women alone possess is the creative power of motherhood, which reflects God's own creative power. Another gift is our emotional depth and sensitivity, which mirror the compassionate mercy of our heavenly Father. Still another is our relational nature. The desire women have to nurture relationships is a reflection of the desire *God* has to nurture relationships. Before Eve appeared on the scene to be in relationship with Adam—and to help bring more human beings into the world—God's image was incomplete.

It's worth spending a little time reflecting on our uniqueness as women. This topic can be emotionally charged for some women, as it was for me, because we carry a fear of being labeled the "weaker sex" or being considered somehow inferior to men. But in his *Letter to Women,* Pope John Paul II put these unfortunate notions to rest. He wrote:

> Woman complements man, just as man complements woman: men and women are *complementary.* Womanhood expresses the "human" as much as manhood does, but in a different and complementary way.... It is only through the duality of the "masculine" and the "feminine" that the "human" finds full realization.[1]

So if the human race lost the "duality" of male and female, humanity would also lose its "full realization." We need men to be men and women to be women if the human race is going to flourish. This is why gender blurring is problematic. Denying the inbuilt uniqueness of men and women leads to serious cultural confusion.

Our Judeo-Christian anthropology insists that the differences between men and women are not merely biological or social constructs. Masculinity and femininity are real distinctions given by God to help us know him better and live fuller, richer lives.

When we strive to become the women God intended us to be, virtuous and spiritually beautiful, we help reveal God to the world. But a woman whose beauty is marred by sin and vice has desecrated the sacred image in which she was made.

Now that we have learned how to be virtuous women, it's important to let the world see just how beautiful God's image can be!

PRAYER

Lord God, thank you for blessing me by making me in your image as a woman. Please help me discover the unique strengths that I possess because of my femininity, and help me use them in the best way possible. Amen.

REFLECTION QUESTIONS

1. Have you always aligned yourself with the Catholic Church? Are there teachings you have struggled with or beliefs that took time to embrace? Where do you stand today?

2. Has anyone ever spoken negatively to you about the Church? How did you handle the situation?

3. Can you think of examples of the blurring of masculinity and femininity in our culture? What are its effects? Have any of these effects touched your life?

4. Does Genesis 1:27 help you understand the dignity of women? Why do you think God chose to reveal his image through the complementary setup of male and female? How could you use this verse to defend the equality of men and women?

5. How often do you think of yourself as bearing God's image to the world? How can you more effectively show God's image to those around you?

Day 29: The Wonder of Women

As I write, my three-month-old baby girl is sleeping next to me in her swing. I can't believe how much I love her.

I had sworn off motherhood back in those days when I had also sworn off "Mother Church." I didn't think I wanted to have children. Even up until three months ago, I still had my doubts! But as soon as Sophia appeared, I wanted to be a mother, *her* mother, more than anything else in the world. Something powerful and undeniable that I used to think was just a myth clicked in me: my maternal nature.

As women we have the *capacity* to bear children, to sustain and nurture new life, to participate in a physical way with God in an act of creation (even if we never use this capacity due to another life calling or a health problem). This ought to leave us in a state of wonder and awe. God chose *women* to work with him in a special way in the act of creation. Our bodies are a sign of this, built as they are to bring new life into the world.

But we are a unity of body and soul. Our souls are also feminine, designed to nurture life and to look out for the well-being of others.

This is why Pope John Paul II used the term "spiritual motherhood" when speaking of the vocation of women. While not every woman will be a physical mother, we all have the gift and calling to nurture human life in other ways. The pope wrote in *On the Dignity and Vocation of Women*: "Spiritual motherhood takes on many different forms....[I]t can express itself as concern for people, especially the most needy: the sick, the handicapped, the abandoned, orphans, the elderly, children, young people, the imprisoned and, in general, people on the edges of society."[2]

Such attentiveness to the needs of others is one of the character istics of a truly beautiful woman. She possesses virtue not only for her own good but for the benefit of others. The virtues of prudence, justice, fortitude, temperance, faith, hope and charity will bear the most fruit when we align them with the particular strengths of our feminine nature.

Defending unborn human life, for example, is harmonious with a woman's nature. A woman dedicated to justice may take this up as a special cause by getting involved in pro-life activities in her community.

Nurturing the spiritual growth of children resonates with our feminine gifts as well. One way a woman can exercise the virtue of faith is by teaching in her parish's religious education program.

Bringing a more "human" perspective to the workplace is also in line with women's inclinations. A woman can exercise the virtue of charity at her workplace by building relationships of trust and warmth. Temperance can help a mother resist the temptation to spend too much time at work to the neglect of her family.

The call to nurture life is a special mission for all women. We can respond by offering physical, emotional and spiritual support to the people God has entrusted to our care. It will be much easier to do this—to respond to our vocation as women—when we cultivate the virtues. These good spiritual habits cooperate to make us more beautiful as individuals, which also helps make the world a more beautiful place to live.

PRAYER

Lord God, I want to embrace my maternal nature. I want to nurture and cultivate life exactly as you would have me do it. Please show me the specific ways I can be a mother to your people. Amen.

REFLECTION QUESTIONS

1. Have you always understood your femininity as a special gift? Has anyone ever made you feel that you were not equal in dignity to a man? What can you do to help the women in your life appreciate their feminine nature?

2. How would you defend the Christian belief that we are a unity of body and soul? What examples could you give to illustrate this reality? What would you say to someone who thinks that a person's gender has nothing to do with the soul?

3. Do you believe that motherhood gets due respect in our culture? How do the legalization of abortion and the promotion of contraception affect society's attitude about maternity? How can you help mothers recognize the importance of their role?

4. Think about some ways that you exercise spiritual maternity within your vocation. What else can you do to put this feminine inclination to good use?

5. Imagine a world without women (impossible, I know). What would it be like? What would be missing? Now imagine a world without men, and ask the same questions. How does this reflection help clarify the idea of complementarity?

Day 30: Growing Good Habits

Every time I go to a hair salon, I come home with some new product or other and the hope of reproducing the fabulous style I just paid for. I am usually diligently dedicated to the new hairdo for a week or so, but before long my latest bottle of mousse, gel, spritzer, cream or spray ends up in a drawer with all the rest of them. The effects of my makeover don't last long when I'm not committed to them.

A spiritual makeover can hit a similar snag. Today we leave the spiritual salon with new excitement and energy, but it will be up to us to make sure our new "look" doesn't fade because of our failure to take care of it. Before this book comes to a close, we would do well to spend a little time talking about how to make our makeover an enduring one.

Popular psychology tells us that it takes thirty days to form a habit. In the course of these thirty days, we have been talking about forming good habits in the seven virtues of prudence, justice, fortitude, temperance, faith, hope and charity and of breaking bad habits of greed, gluttony, lust, sloth, envy, anger and pride. I suspect that merely presenting these ideas doesn't equal the practice psychologists recommend. The process of forming good habits doesn't end here; in fact, this is only the beginning.

Developing these virtues will take time and effort. Don't be discouraged if you find yourself struggling with them; that's a natural part of the process. When in our weakness we fall into temptation and sin, it's up to us to stand up again and move forward instead of being defeated and giving up. All we need to do is sincerely seek forgiveness from God and anyone we may have hurt and resolve to do better in the future.

The sacrament of reconciliation helps with this task. Jesus gave us this sacrament to restore our relationship with God after we sin and to provide us with supernatural help to do better the next time.

As you become more aware of the vices you struggle with, you may want to focus specific attention on particular virtues. A helpful tool for making quick progress is to focus on one virtue a month. We can use the thirty-day method to form good habits.

At the end of this book, you will find thirty-day charts for all seven virtues. Suppose you choose temperance this month because you have a tendency to overeat. You can make a specific goal, such as "Eat only two cookies each day," or more generally, "Do not eat more than I need." Mark your progress in self-control: if you make it through the first day without giving in to gluttony, circle the "1" on your chart; if you eat too many chocolate chip cookies tomorrow, put a slash through the "2" and so on. You will quickly become conscious of your goal this way. After thirty days you will be surprised how much easier it is to have two cookies instead of four.

This method of forming one good habit at a time has a much greater chance of success than trying to do everything at once. But remember that even the best "method" for self-improvement will never be completely effective without God's supernatural grace. Praying for God's strength to help us develop virtue should be part of our everyday routine. We also have the opportunity to receive graces through the sacraments. Going to monthly confession and receiving Communion regularly will benefit us as we seek to grow in the fullness of beauty.

By now you have formed a habit of setting aside a little time each day to read this book and to answer the reflection questions. Now that you're in a rhythm, you might consider utilizing this time to maintain the effects of your spiritual makeover. Perhaps you could attend morning Mass or meditate on the Gospel reading for the day. Or you could commit the time to spiritual reading and prayer.

Whatever you decide to do from this point forward, remember that it's up to you to preserve the effects of your makeover. You could walk into a salon today, get a fabulous new haircut and color, a manicure and a facial, but if you fail to wash your hair, touch up your nails or take care of your skin, the effects of the makeover won't last long. Similarly, to preserve our spiritual beauty, we wash off the dirt by asking Christ's forgiveness in reconciliation, we get a touch-up through receiving him in the Eucharist, and we take care of our souls by being in daily contact with Jesus through prayer.

Jesus was perfectly virtuous, after all. The people who reflect his virtue most beautifully—the saints—have done so by keeping in close contact with him. They radiate authentic beauty as a result. And you and I are called to embrace and reflect that very same magnificent beauty here on earth.

PRAYER

Lord God, please help me carry out my spiritual resolutions. When my human motivation begins to wane, supply me with divine grace. I want to become a new creation with your help and reveal true beauty to the world. Amen.

REFLECTION QUESTIONS

1. Can you relate to the tendency to let a makeover—or a resolution —slide? When have you failed to follow through on a personal commitment? Why do you think it happened? What can you do to make sure this spiritual makeover "sticks"?

2. Review the resolutions you have made over the course of these thirty days. How would you rate your progress? What ideas and resolutions have been most helpful to you throughout this process?

3. Which of the virtues are you most excited about cultivating? Why do you think these stand out for you?

4. Think about the lives of your favorite saints. Can you identify specific virtues they possessed? How can their examples be helpful to you in your quest to develop virtue?

5. Consider writing a short prayer that you can pray each morning, asking God to help you as you strive to grow in beauty and holiness.

SUGGESTED SPIRITUAL ACTIVITY

Understanding womanhood in the light of our Catholic faith brings clarity and joy in a sometimes confused world. Why not invest a little time in some reading that will help you embrace your nature and identity as a woman? *Consider reading Pope John Paul II's Apostolic Exhortation* Mulieris Dignitatem, *On the Dignity and Vocation of Women.*

PERSONAL REFLECTION AND RESOLUTION

My thoughts about this chapter:

My resolution:

Models of Victory

MARY

This humble handmaid has been "exalted by the Lord as Queen of the universe,"[3] as we recall in the fifth glorious mystery of the rosary. The book of Revelation describes the heavenly grandeur of Mary, the mother of our Savior, a "woman clothed with the sun, with the moon under her feet, and on her head a crown of twelve stars" (Revelation 12:1). What a remarkable destiny for someone who never sought any glory for herself!

Mary's choice to follow God's will led her to the piercing sorrows and tragic trials of her son's passion and death. Yet she emerged victorious alongside her son and now enjoys eternal happiness in his company. And even in her celestial glory, Mary continues to direct her faithful children to Jesus. Her mission is his mission, her glory is his glory, and her victory is the victory that Christ won for all of us: the victory over sin and death.

Mary knew she wasn't holy by her own power; God's grace preserved her from sin. So too we are not meant to be alone in our pursuit of virtue. Not only does God want to walk with each one of his beloved daughters, but Mary accompanies us too. How blessed we are to have such exalted company on our quest for virtue!

THE COMMUNION OF SAINTS

Everyone in the glorious communion of saints is a model of victory. The stories of the countless women and men in heaven, vastly diverse as they are, all involve the inevitable battle between virtue and vice. The particular struggles, the specific temptations, the individual trials they faced differ greatly: Some had dramatic conversions from serious patterns of sin; others were faithful all their lives, even in the face of personal weaknesses; still others vacillated between saintliness and sinfulness as they sought to become holy. But all of them emerged victorious, finally united to Christ in spite of the obstacles along the way.

Just as their difficulties varied, so too they cultivated the virtues in response to the unique situations in their lives. Some saints were masters of courage, some perfected the virtue of temperance, and others had a burning charity in their hearts. No matter what virtue we may want to develop, these brothers and sisters in Christ can help us by both their example and their intercession.

Virtuous Victories

These charts can help you form new habits of virtue one at a time. Select the chart for the virtue that you want to develop this month. Establish a particular goal for each, such as "I will not gossip," for the virtue of justice. Review your day each evening, and give yourself either a circle (for victory) or a slash (for defeat). At the end of the month, you will be able to see your progress!

month:		virtue: prudence			
specific goal:					
1	2	3	4	5	6
7	8	9	10	11	12
13	14	15	16	17	18
19	20	21	22	23	24
25	26	27	28	29	30

month:		virtue: justice			
specific goal:					
1	2	3	4	5	6
7	8	9	10	11	12
13	14	15	16	17	18
19	20	21	22	23	24
25	26	27	28	29	30

month:		virtue: fortitude			
specific goal:					
1	2	3	4	5	6
7	8	9	10	11	12
13	14	15	16	17	18
19	20	21	22	23	24
25	26	27	28	29	30

month:	virtue: *temperance*
specific goal:	

1	2	3	4	5	6
7	8	9	10	11	12
13	14	15	16	17	18
19	20	21	22	23	24
25	26	27	28	29	30

month:	virtue: *faith*
specific goal:	

1	2	3	4	5	6
7	8	9	10	11	12
13	14	15	16	17	18
19	20	21	22	23	24
25	26	27	28	29	30

month:	virtue: *hope*
specific goal:	

1	2	3	4	5	6
7	8	9	10	11	12
13	14	15	16	17	18
19	20	21	22	23	24
25	26	27	28	29	30

month:	virtue: *charity*
specific goal:	

1	2	3	4	5	6
7	8	9	10	11	12
13	14	15	16	17	18
19	20	21	22	23	24
25	26	27	28	29	30

Bibliography

Books and Church Documents

Catherine of Siena. *The Dialogue*. New York: Paulist, 1980.

Christian Prayer: The Liturgy of the Hours. New York: Catholic Book, 1976.

Corrigan, Felicitas, ed. *The Saints, Humanly Speaking*. Ann Arbor, Mich.: Servant, 2000.

Escrivá, Josemaría. *The Way, Furrow, The Forge*. Princeton, N.J.: Scepter, 1998.

Gauthier, Jacques. *I Thirst: Saint Thérèse of Lisieux and Mother Teresa of Calcutta*. Staten Island, N.Y.: Society of St. Paul, 2005.

Lewis, C.S. *The Beloved Works of C.S. Lewis*. Grand Rapids, Mich.: Family Christian, 1960.

Mother Teresa. *The Joy in Loving: A Guide to Daily Living with Mother Teresa*. Compiled by Jaya Chalika and Edward Le Joly. New York: Penguin Compass, 1996.

Pontifical Council for the Family. *The Truth and Meaning of Human Sexuality: Guidelines for Education within the Family*. www.vatican.va.

Pope John Paul II. *Centesimus Annus*. www.vatican.va.

_____ . *The Dignity and Vocation of Women*. www.vatican.va.

_____ . *Evangelium Vitae*. www.vatican.va.

_____ . *Letter to Women*. www.vatican.va.

_____ . *Mother of the Redeemer*. www.vatican.va.

Second Vatican Council. *Lumen Gentium*. www.vatican.va.

Sisters of Mercy, trans., *A Year With the Saints: Twelve Christian Virtues in the Lives and Writings of the Saints*. Rockford, Ill.: Tan, 1988.

Teresa of Avila. *The Life of Saint Teresa of Avila by Herself*. J.M. Cohen, trans. London: Penguin, 1988.

Web Sites

www.americancatholic.org

www.catholicity.com

www.catholicnews.com

www.ewtn.com

www.newadvent.org

www.servantbooks.org

www.therealpresence.org

Notes

Chapter One: Choosing Beauty

1. *Christian Prayer: The Liturgy of the Hours* (New York: Catholic Book, 1976), p. 1336.
2. Pope John Paul II, *Mother of the Redeemer*, no. 46, available at: www.vatican.va.
3. Pope John Paul II, *Letter to Women*, no. 10, available at: www.vatican.va.
4. Pope John Paul II, Angelus Address, July 23, 1995, available at: www.ewtn.com.
5. Pope John Paul II, *Letter to Women*, no. 12.

Chapter Two: Prudence

1. Thomas Aquinas, *Summa Theologica* II–II, ques. 47, art. 2, quoted at www.newadvent.org.
2. Catherine dei Ricci, "Letter to Prato," in Felicitas Corrigan, ed., *The Saints, Humanly Speaking* (Ann Arbor, Mich.: Servant, 2000), p. 245.
3. Second Vatican Council, *Dignitatis Humanae*, Declaration on Religious Freedom.

Chapter Three: Justice

1. Pope John Paul II, *Centesimus Annus*, no. 58, available at: www.vatican.va.
2. *A Year With the Saints: Twelve Christian Virtues in the Lives and Writings of the Saints*, Sisters of Mercy, trans. (Rockford, Ill.: Tan, 1988), p. 264.
3. Brandon Hatfield, "Statue symbolizes justice for the poor and oppressed," quoted at www.rensselaerrepublican.com.

Chapter Four: Fortitude

1. Pope John Paul II, *Evangelium Vitae*, no. 12, available at: www.vatican.va.
2. Pope Benedict XVI, Homily for the Mass of Installation, April 2005, available at: www.catholicnews.com.

Chapter Five: Temperance

1. Pontifical Council for the Family, *The Truth and Meaning of Human Sexuality: Guidelines for Education within the Family*, no. 16, available at: www.vatican.va.

Chapter Six: Faith

1. *Dei Verbum* is the Vatican II document on divine revelation.
2. Josemaría Escrivá, *The Way, Furrow, The Forge* (Princeton, N.J.: Scepter, 1998), p. 325.
3. Escrivá, p. 621.

4. Melvin L. Farrell, trans., "Humbly Let Us Voice Our Homage," available at: www.therealpresence.org.

5. "Saints Perpetua and Felicity," available at: www.ewtn.com.

Chapter Seven: Hope

1. J.M. Cohen, trans., *The Life of Saint Teresa of Avila by Herself* (London: Penguin, 1957), p. 63.

2. Jacques Gauthier, *I Thirst: Thérèse of Lisieux and Mother Teresa*, Alexandra Plettenberg-Serban, trans. (Staten Island, N.Y.: Society of St. Paul, 2005), p. 73.

3. Mother Teresa, *The Joy in Loving: A Guide to Daily Living with Mother Teresa*, Jaya Chalika and Edward Le Joly, comps. (New York: Penguin Compass, 1996), p. 65.

Chapter Eight: Charity

1. Catherine of Siena, *The Dialogue*, Suzanne Noffke, O.P., trans. (New York: Paulist, 1980), p. 118.

2. C.S. Lewis, *The Four Loves*, in *The Beloved Works of C.S. Lewis* (Grand Rapids, Mich.: Family Christian, 1960), p. 244.

3. *Dialogue*, p. 121; see Matthew 25:40.

Chapter Nine: Virtue Versus Vice

1. Vatican II, *Lumen Gentium*, no. 11, in Austin Flannery, ed., *Vatican Council II: The Conciliar and Post Conciliar Documents* (Northport, N.Y.: Costello, 1996), vol. 1, p. 362.

Chapter Ten: Virtuous Womanhood

1. Pope John Paul II, *Letter to Women*, no. 7.

2. Pope John Paul II, *Mulieris Dignitatem*, no. 21, available at: www.vatican.va.

3. Vatican II, *Lumen Gentium*, no. 59, available at: www.ewtn.com.